How Bad Do You Want It?
It's Time to P.U.S.H.!

Regina G. Mixon & Evangelist Lavina Williams

HOW BAD DO YOU WANT IT?
IT'S TIME TO P.U.S.H.!!!

ISBN978-1-64008-500-8

Published by:

REGS Books Publishing

P. O. Box 5397

Torrance, CA 90510

All scriptures quoted are KJV unless specified otherwise.

Library of Congress Cataloging-in-Publication Data

Mixon, Regina G. 1957-

Williams, Lavina

Printed in the United States of America

Contents

FOREWORD

It is truly an honor and a privilege to write this foreword, not only because Regina Mixon and Evangelist Lavina Williams are great friends of mine, but because they are true missionaries of our Lord and Savior, Jesus Christ. They have hearts of gold for the women of God. They want you to win in every area of your life! This very sentiment resonates in my spirit. I, too, believe deeply in women and want them to win in every area of their lives. You can do all things through Christ who strengthens you (Philippians 4:13); but the question that must be answered is, "How Bad Do <u>You</u> Want It?"

Notice the word "<u>you</u>" is underlined. It is highlighted because action is required to achieve the desires of your heart. This book, written by two amazing women, offers biblical strategies combined with **real life** experiences to show how you can accomplish the things you want to accomplish *if* you want them badly enough. Push past all the excuses, get in the race of your life, and we'll see you at the finish line!

Karen" KJ" Johnson
Global Brand Strategist
Executive Director, Dress for Success, Dallas

CREDITS/ACKNOWLEDGEMENTS

I would like to acknowledge the MVP for all my life, my mother Joyce Gilbert. Momma, I love you! It feels so good to make you proud. Because of you, I am who I am!

I would like to acknowledge my husband, Deacon Tommy Williams. Thank you, husband, for encouraging and supporting me in ministry. I love you!

I would like to acknowledge my sons, Damien Sr., Bobby Jr., and Cameron. I love you young men and I feel blessed to be your mother. I am proud of all three of you and I know that God has great things in store for you.

I would like to acknowledge my pastor, Dr. Rodney E. Williams, for all that you have taught me throughout the near 20 years I have been under your leadership. Thank you for being a great example, for all your support, and for being the best pastor in the world.

I would like to acknowledge my Spiritual Mother, Regina Mixon. Thank you for pushing me to do more and for giving me opportunities to do that. Thanks to you, I have the new title: author. This is just the beginning!

Evangelist Lavina D. Williams

I would like to acknowledge, first and foremost, my two amazing children, Kendrick J. Thomas and Emily N. Mixon, and my awesome and amazingly gregarious grandson, Jordan D. Gilliam. We may not be perfect, but God blessed us to be a perfect fit for each other.

I would like to acknowledge my aunt, Bertha Richardson Mitchell, who has been there with me from day one acting in many different roles as my aunt, best friend, confidante, leaning post, sounding board, big sister, and so much more. I will always love you.

I would like to acknowledge each and every one of my family members. I say thank you. Although it took me some time to realize this, God blessed me with His best in giving me the gift of each of you.

I would like to acknowledge my current pastor, Dr. Rodney E. Williams, for your leadership, guidance, direction, support, and prayers. Thank you for believing in me when many others did not. I am eternally grateful.

I would like to acknowledge my past pastors who poured into my life over this 20-year period of learning, growing, falling, and getting back up. Pastor W. Terrell Snead, II, Pastor Ron C. Hill, and Bishop Noel Jones, I thank each of you so much for your great leadership, your teachings, and for allowing me to use my gifts. Thank you for your prayers.

I would like to acknowledge my amazing editor, Trease Shine. It is so rare to find someone so supportive, someone who catches the vision and runs with it, someone who does such an incredible job. You, my friend, are priceless!

I would like to acknowledge Karen "KJ" Johnson, my sister from other parents, my partner when I need a great laugh, my Branding Coach, and so much more. Forever and always, we are sisters! I have learned so much from you.

I would like to acknowledge my health and wellness coach, Felicia R. Phillips. Because of you, I believed I could, and I did. Your encouragement and support were infectious. I believed I could fly, you reinforced that belief, and I am still soaring. Thank you for your prayers and last, but not least, your friendship.

I would like to acknowledge my entire Women Destined to Win International Community. Because of you and your support, because of your continued words of encouragement, because of your sharing information and resources, I have written this book.

I would like to give special acknowledgement to my administrators, most of whom have been with me for the past three years: Janet R. Tate, Forya Calloway, Evangelist Lavina D. Williams, Carlene Ebanks Graham, Chantay Denson Nicholson, Kinedia Brown-Diggs, Minister Beverly Siah-Hulbin, Rose Terral, Sherylee Warr, Alice Marie Leftridge, Shiemetre Smith, and Mary Banos.

My Official Prayer Team: Lady Regina Poole, Evangelist Sandra R. Hamilton, Kaldejia "Lady Dee" Faulk, Karen "KJ" Johnson, Nikki Carcisse-Patterson, Lady Rebecca D. Huggins, Chandra B. Payne, Evangelist Lavina D. Williams, Minister Beverly Siah-Hulbin, Yolanda Richburg, Lady Tina DeLoach, Evangelist Gennell Lofton, and Pastor Jessie Faye Manuel.

Last, but not least, I acknowledge my Spiritual Daughter, Evangelist Lavina D. Williams, for seeing something in me that she deemed so worthy, she asked that I serve as her Spiritual Mother. It goes without saying, I have been, and continue to be, both honored and humbled. To God be all glory.

Regina G. Mixon

DEDICATION

I dedicate my portion of this book to my Lord Jesus, who I love with all of my heart and my grandchildren: Damien Jr., Carmen, Kevin, Journee, Reese, and Phoebe.

In memory of my grandmother, Lillie Mae Flucas.

Evangelist Lavina D. Williams

I dedicate this portion of my book in memory of my dearly departed friends, Renee Givhan and Kay Dianne Walker Cary Caesar.

It was an honor to have met Renee, serving alongside her in the Christian Education Department at Love & Unity Christian Fellowship in Compton, CA. Renee was an amazing woman, full of love for God, her family, and others.

Kay was a phenomenal woman, a real mover and shaker, a woman who spoke her mind, but loved God with her entire mind, body, and soul.

To the both of you, we often say that one has left too soon, but God wants His best too. The angels in heaven are rejoicing while we are saddened by the great void left. Each of you will forever be in my heart. I love you.

Regina G. Mixon

To God be the GLORY!

INTRODUCTION

How Bad Do YOU Want It?

It's Time to P.U.S.H.

At various stages in our lives, we must decide how badly we really want something. There is always a price to pay in order to attain that which we desire.

Seasons change. Sometimes what *was* will not fit in our new season. In order to get what we want; it is sometimes necessary to let go of what was.

We cannot hold on to what *was* while reaching for a new thing. In the book of James, it states that a double-minded man is unstable in all his ways. *"But let him ask in faith, with no doubting; for he who doubts is like a wave of the sea driven and tossed by the wind.8 For let not that man suppose that he will receive anything from the Lord; he is a double-minded man, unstable in all his ways." (New King James Version, James 1:6-8)*

To move into a new season, there are some things we absolutely must do. Allow Evangelist Lavina Williams and me to share some things with you, from a Biblical perspective *and* a practical perspective, that you can begin to do immediately. Start to P. U. S. H. and walk into the new thing that God wants to do for you.

There is always a price to pay for one's freedom. Are you now ready to pay the price? Wishing won't make it happen. Faith alone won't make it happen. It is time to do the work! It is time to P. U. S. H. and give birth to whatever it is God has placed inside you.

FROM THE PEN OF REGINA

"How Bad Do You Want It?

It's Time to P. U. S. H.

"If a problem can be solved with action, you don't have a problem."

-Mel Robbins

The decision we are often confronted with is how bad do we really want something or to see changes take place in our lives. These decisions can be exciting initially, but after some time has passed, and some steps have been taken, sometimes the excitement will leave. Decisions to do something or go after something requires change.

We have to change our mindsets, our thoughts, our circles, sometimes even our geographical locations. We have to change our habits. We have to move from "stinking thinking" to power thoughts. We have to encourage ourselves, look for, and connect with like-minded people who will encourage us along the journey.

We must disconnect from some family members and friends. This can be very painful, but is often necessary.

My portion of this book will speak to the "how bad do you want changes in your life" questions you may have. These solutions relate to living a peace-filled life, having a healthier lifestyle, financial freedom, breaking destructive habits, restoring relationships, and other areas that need to be addressed.

I will primarily deal with the importance of properly **preparing**, of having the necessary **patience**, and the necessity of **partnership** (when it's needed) in order to accomplish your desired results.

One definition of insanity is to keep doing things the same way while expecting different results. That is not the season we are in. Our desire is to truly be all that God has called us to be and we will settle for nothing less.

We were not created to live mediocre lifestyles, but to SHINE for God's glory. We were not created to settle for less than God's best, but to live an ABUNDANT lifestyle. We were not created to live with poor relationships, in lack and poverty, in poor health. God's word lets us know that.

In this writing, I will be totally candid about some things I have experienced in hopes that you, too, can experience some breakthroughs in your life and are able to BREAK FREE!

And they overcame him by the blood of the Lamb, and by the word of their testimony; and they loved not their lives unto the death. (King James Bible, Rev. 12:11)

CHAPTER ONE

A RELATIONSHIP WITH GOD – Lavina D. Williams

Everything changed in 2020. The world suffered a hard reset that was more devastating than we could have imagined. God had our attention, if but for a time! When many people got over their fear of the world ending, they went back to doing what they were doing before the pandemic. But for the remnants, of God everything changed! I often say, I lost my religion in 2020!

I had a Tent Crusade scheduled for April that had to be cancelled because of the Covid 19 restrictions against gatherings larger than 10 people. As a result of the cancellation, I chose to hold it virtually, but scaled it down to one speaker. One major point that the teacher made in her teaching was that we should make time to sit in the presence of the Lord daily. So, the next morning I began to do just that. I set my alarm to rise early and commune with God at the start of my day and every day thereafter. That my friends, was the beginning of my dramatically transformed, mind blowing relationship with the Lord. No cliché - My life has not been the same since that day! I realized I had to be in the presence of God every day. The more I met with Him, the more He talked to me and revealed things to me.

One Saturday morning, I woke up totally drained of all my energy. It took all my strength to get up and make my way to my prayer room, but I was determined to get in the presence of the Lord. I didn't know what was going on with me, I had only felt so weak when I had the flu, but I was not sick. I had an appointment scheduled for late morning, but I knew that I would have to reschedule it. I made my way to my prayer room where I prayed and read my Bible. As I read, I said, "Lord, I'm going to lay back down", but I didn't move right away. I continued to read in Ezekiel and David was mentioned, and I saw how God honored him even in death. I do realize that David, in some texts of scripture, is a typology of Christ; however, the way God continued to honor him as He promised He would, was just so loving. I said, "Lord, you really loved David" and He replied, "I love you, too, just as much!" At that moment, I felt His love pour out on me and I was overwhelmed! It was an intimate encounter. I literally felt His love for me! It was so intense, and His glory was so heavy. When I left that room, I did not have to go lay back down. I was energized and ready to do what God had told me to do. Whatever was going on in my body could not stay in the presence of God! I am now convinced that whatever ailment you may have, if you get in the glorious presence of the Lord, you will be healed and changed. In His presence is the fulness of joy! I feel that He only poured out as much as I could handle!

The same experience that I had on that day, is available for you. God has no respect of persons. He showed me that He didn't love David who was a man after His own heart any more than He loves me, and He doesn't love me any more than He loves you. He wants to pour His love out on you, too! All you have to do is make yourself available to Him. Don't be so busy that you don't make time for the Lord. He is a jealous God, and He will have no one or nothing before Him. Begin to prioritize your day so that you can set a special time for you and Holy Ghost to fellowship. Set the time for when there are no other things pulling at you and demanding your attention. I like to meet with Him early in the mornings because my mind is fresh and starting the day with Holy Ghost makes it so much better. David said, in Psalm 63:1 (*American King James Version*) *O God, you are my God; Early will I seek You: my soul thirsts for You; my flesh longs for you in a dry and thirsty land, where no water is.* David is expressing in the psalm that there is nothing that can fill or quench ones thirst like the refreshing presence of the Lord. He will satisfy your thirsty soul like nothing else in this world! The more you get in the presence of God, the more you will want to. Your appetite for Him will increase more and more. Job said, I have not departed from the commandment of His lips; I have treasured the words of His mouth more than my necessary food. (Job 23:12 *New King James Version*) When your appetite for Jesus increases, your desire for other things will decrease! Fellowship is just as important to Him as it is for you. Fellowship can be anything from a small group outing to even outside events. He loves you so much and He wants your time and attention.

"Relationship" is a word that has taken the modern church by storm in a good way. It is what God is calling us back to — a relationship with Him. We have learned how to do church well. We know the protocols, we know the lingo, we know how to dance and shout, but do we really know God? God is not seeking robots but true worshippers! He wants you to know Him! Jesus told the woman at the well, "Ye worship ye know not what: we know what we worship: for salvation is of the Jews. But the hour cometh, and now is, when the true worshippers shall worship the Father in spirit and in truth: for the Father seeketh such to worship Him." (*John 4:22-23 King James Version*) True worshippers get to know Him! Don't be guilty of being present at all the church events and not even know the God of the church. You should go to church, but going to church does not take the place of a personal relationship with the Lord. God is saying, "Know Me!" You can't truly know someone you never talk to! Getting to know someone is a continual process. It is impossible to know everything about God, but as we walk with

Him, we learn more about Him. He not only wants to dwell in temples made with the hands of man, but He also wants to dwell in you the temple made with His hands! He doesn't need anything from you, seeing that he giveth to all life, and breath, and all things. He desires a relationship with you. There is nothing you can offer to Him that will please Him like the offering of yourself. *Hosea 6: 6 New*

Living Translation, says "I want you to show love, not offer sacrifices. I want you to know me more than I want burnt offerings." In essence, God is saying, I don't want your sacrifices—I want your love; I don't want your offerings—I want you to know me. He wants you more than anything that you offer Him. For in him we live and move, and have our being, for we are also his offspring. He is not a man-made god, but He is the creator of the heavens and the earth. He is our Heavenly Father who created us from the dust of the ground. He gave us life! No good father has children and then makes them fend for themselves! He is the only Father that will not precede us. He is there for all time. So, we ought not to treat the Godhead like an idol---something that we can pick up and put down when we get ready.

We must be careful not to put religion before relationship. Religion is only bad when it is alone, like faith and works. Relationship is faith, religion is works. James talks about pure, undefiled religion, so it's not a bad thing, just make sure it's not all you have. Some replace their intimacy with the Lord with service to the church and/or leaders. If you put house cleaning or yard work in the place of intimacy with your spouse, then there would be some warrantable problems in your marriage. Jesus wants you even if you don't want Him and He will not stop pursuing you as long as you live.

God is very open and honest about His feelings for you, and He expresses that in the Bible consistently. He is all-in and He proved it when He gave His only begotten Son to die for you! He loves you with an everlasting love and He wants a one-on-one relationship with you. You can commune with Him even when words fail you. He sees the heart, and He knows your intentions and motives, so even when you don't know what to say, you can go to Him. The Bible says that the Spirit helps our infirmities: for we know not what we should pray for as we ought: but the Spirit itself makes intercession for us with groanings that cannot be uttered. (*Romans 8:26 King James Version*)

Prayer is your conversation with God. When my grandson learned to talk, I taught him simple prayers so that He would get used to praying to God even though he didn't understand. When he turned 7 years old, I began teaching him how to pray unrehearsed, unmemorized prayers. He started his first prayer in this fashion, "Hey God, how are you doing?" Honestly, I thought you don't ask God how He is doing. You know how He is doing - "He's good!" Nevertheless, I did not try to correct him or make him think he was praying wrong because it was his conversation with the Lord, not mine. However, as I thought about it later, I said to myself, *"Wow, I never thought to ask God how He was doing,* but that is a totally relevant question for Him. He has feelings, not like ours but feelings nonetheless and when you approach someone, you generally greet them first.

Prayer is our primary method of communication with the Father. Some people believe that if God is all-knowing, why should we pray? We pray because prayer is a mighty weapon and a key of the Kingdom of Heaven. We pray because Jesus said that if we ask anything in His Name, He will do it. We pray because the effectual fervent prayer of the righteous avails much. *And this is the confidence that we have in Him, that, if we ask any thing according to His will, He heareth us: And if we know that He hear us, whatsoever we ask, we know that we have the petitions that we desired of Him. (1 John 5:14-15 King James Version)* Jesus gave us a model prayer that teaches us how to approach Father God, how to reverence Him, and how to petition Him for what we desire. When you pray, you don't have to have perfect words or speak to Him in Greek, Hebrew, or in King James English. Just pour out your heart to Him because that's what He wants - your heart. If you can't find the words to say, you can pray the Word of God, laid out in the Bible. He said to bring Him in remembrance of His Word. There are promises in the Word that you should claim and confess. The promises are already yours, but you have to stake your claim and take ownership of them.

We have been given exceedingly great and precious promises. All the promises of God are in Him, yea, and in Him, Amen. It is written and it shall be done. God is not a man that He should lie; neither the son of man, that he should repent: hath he said, and shall he not do it? Or hath he spoken, and shall he not make it good? (*Numbers 23:19 King James Version*) He will do what He said, and He will make it good for you, if you just trust Him!

You should delight yourself in the Lord and in your relationship with Him. To "delight in" means to be very happy because of something, to enjoy something very much. When you delight yourself in the Lord, you make Him supreme in your life. You find joy in going before Him, resting in Him, and walking with Him daily. When you delight in God, He delights in you! He takes joy in fellowshipping with you.

When God starts something in you, He starts with the end in mind. He doesn't half-do anything. When He led the children of Israel out of Egypt, He already had the Promised Land for them. Even though disobedience delayed them, God still provided for them in the wilderness. You may be in the wilderness, but God is still providing for you. He is faithful to fulfill every promise. Just don't die in the wilderness! Don't die on your way to the promise! God made a way of salvation for you because He wanted your end to be better than your beginning. He knows the thoughts that He thinks toward you, thoughts of peace and not of evil, to give you an expected end. Your expected end was projected when you accepted Jesus as your Savior and Lord.

The wilderness is an uncultivated place not meant for permanent habitation. It's not a place to settle in and take up residence. The wilderness is for tents not houses. Don't get comfortable on your journey through the wilderness. Keep the vision of the promise fresh before you. *Habakkuk 2:2-3 King James Version* says, And the Lord answered me and said, Write the vision, and make it plain upon tables, that he may run that readeth it. For the vision is yet for an appointed time, but at the end it shall speak, and not lie: though it tarry, wait for it; because it will surely come, it will not tarry." The vision is what God told you and showed you. Write it down, draw a diagram, or make a vision board and keep it at hand's reach so that it will motivate you to keep moving. God is pleased when you trust Him to bring it to pass. God is your compass through the wilderness, and He will lead you into the place of promise - you just need to be obedient and trust Him.

One of the things the Lord told me was that He is Father and not a slave master. He said, "I want relationship, not to give you bondage!" There are so many people in bondage to religion. There is a difference between faithful service and bondage. I am a faithful member of my church, and throughout the years, I have had to examine my heart and evaluate my service to assure that I am not more faithful to my church than I am to God. You should be a faithful member of your church and be subject to your pastor, but don't value your service to the church over your devotion to God!

Many years ago, I worked at a plant on an assembly line. I had been employed there for several months before the line that I was hired to work on shut down. I was then placed on another line that I was never trained on. Less than a week after I started on the line, a gentleman who had been hired to troubleshoot and improve production, was calling me into his office to talk to me about my low production. Before I went in, I thought to myself, "I just started working on this line, I haven't gotten the hang of it yet." At that moment, the Holy Ghost said, "Shhhhh, don't say a word." I went in when I was called, and the gentleman talked to me and offered a solution to my issue, and I rendered no defense in obedience to the Holy Ghost. I listened to his lecture and agreed with his suggestions. However, I was later laid off from that job. Years later, I saw a nursery worker position listed in the classifieds, and I was interested but I did not inquire about the position. Several weeks later, I was checking the classified section again seeking a job, and the job was still listed, and I thought to myself, the Lord must have this job for me. So, I called to inquire about the job, and was encouraged to come in to apply. I went to the church and met with the pastor and his wife. I felt the pastor's wife sizing me up in the spirit. It was clear to me that this job would not be given to just anyone. I shared with her that I had no prior experience working with children but that I did have experience with my own three children. Later, the pastor's wife called me and said that the job would be given to either me or another young lady who had experience working with children. After a few weeks she called to inform me that the job would be given to the other young lady because of her experience. I still felt like the Lord held that job for me, but she got it. Approximately six weeks later, I received a call from the pastor's wife saying that the other young lady had resigned and that the job was mine if I was still interested. Needless to say, I took the job because I felt like this was what the Lord wanted me to do. I later found out that the gentleman-troubleshooter at the plant who called me in about my low production was a pastor and a friend of the pastor of the church that hired me. They said that he spoke well of me, and this somewhat sealed the deal for them to hire me. I did not know that gentleman before our meeting and had no other interaction with him while we worked at the same plant. His impression of me was borne out of my obedience to the Holy Ghost that day. The jobs I mentioned may seem menial to some, but that one act of obedience on my part opened the door for promises fulfilled. Today, after all those years, I still benefit from that one simple act of obedience. Obedience is the key to promised victory. If the Lord tells you to do something, do it. He speaks to us in different ways, and as you learn His ways, you will learn His voice and vice-versa. When you know for sure that it was Him, make it a practice to instantly obey His instructions. Don't wait around for sign after sign. Just simply do what He says. The Bible says that obedience is better that sacrifice. He values your obedience more than your acts of worship. Can you imagine your mother telling you to take out the trash and you offer her a compliment instead? What is more important in that moment? Not the offering of the compliment but your obedience. If you be willing and obedient you will eat the good of the land.

You are blessed and no one can curse you. In Numbers, Balak wanted Balaam to curse the children of Israel, but God had blessed them, and it could not be reversed. God will not change His mind about you no matter who doesn't like you. What He has spoken and declared for your life is secure! You belong to Him, and He will make it good for you. I encourage you to chase the presence of God and be tenacious like Jacob - don't let Him go till He blesses you! The kingdom of heaven suffereth violence and the violent take it by force. How you seek His face reveals how bad you want a relationship with Him.

CHAPTER TWO

PEACE OF MIND – Regina G. Mixon

"Destiny is not a matter of chance, but rather choice."
-William Jennings Bryan

Peace of mind is priceless! Amid all the noise of the world, we can still have peace. In the New International Version of John 14:27, Jesus said "Peace I leave with you, my peace I give to you, I do not give you as the world gives. Do not let your hearts be troubled and do not be afraid."

Isaiah 26:3 (*King James Version*) states, *"Thou will keep him in perfect peace, whose mind is stayed on thee, because he trusteth in thee."*

You may say, "Okay you've given me scriptures, but how can I practically apply these to my life when all hell is breaking loose? Theoretically it sounds great, but how do I get and maintain peace of mind? Please tell me how!"

Well, the secret is not really a big secret. Look at the word of God shown above. One of the things Jesus has left us as an inheritance is peace. Not just peace, but perfect peace. What then, is the secret to obtaining this perfect peace? As we train our focus on our problem-solver as opposed to whatever situation or troubles we are faced with — as we shift our thinking — as we think about all the good in our lives, we can live a life filled with peace.

I did not know this for many years and because of that I suffered unnecessarily. As a "controller" who is now in recovery, I find myself relapsing from time-to-time. The difference between now and then for me is back then, it took days, weeks, months, or even years to get over a thing, now my peace is restored within minutes or a few hours at the longest. I learned to shift.

Believe me, I have had plenty of opportunities to allow my peace of mind to be disturbed—plenty! Just like you, I have had some major, life-changing events throughout the years. Raising children, married, divorced, remarried "several times", going through health issues, dealing with rebellious children, returning to school, work, falling, getting back up, and trying to handle other's business when I wasn't even taking care of my own. You name it, I've seen it and done it!

There were periods of times in my life when I allowed things to overwhelm me to the point that I had absolutely no idea which way to turn or which way to go. In some instances, I sought help, but sometimes found myself misinformed, or I failed to apply many of the recommendations toward a solution to the problem.

I fought with myself, I fought with the enemy, and I fought with God.

I prayed, cried, and did everything to find that peace I so desperately desired, craved, and needed, but to no avail. I'm telling you I did some of everything. Then as I began to pray and meditate on God's word, I realized that God wants us whole—nothing missing, and nothing broken. He wants us to live an abundant life in *all* areas. He wants us to have love, joy, peace, happiness, and every good thing. He died for us to have an abundant life.

3 John 2 *(King James Version)* states, "Beloved I wish above all things that thou mayest prosper and be in health, even as thy soul prospereth. He wants us to have total life prosperity.

You may say that you don't believe in the Bible, the word of God. That is perfectly okay; however, I am sharing with you what works for me. If you don't believe, I encourage you to try it—you just might find that The Word truly does work.

Are there things that have taken place in your life that, you feel are hindering your ability to live in peace today? Let's look at some different scenarios and move toward eliminating those feelings that are preventing you from living the peaceful life of your dreams. I don't want you to have any excuses. Here are a few scenarios.

You're working on a very demanding job. Your supervisor is very demanding. In addition to this, your home life is in shambles. Your husband doesn't understand the pressure you're under, the children are in so many activities that even with your planner, you find yourself missing important events.

The pressure is mounting and appears to be more than you can bear. That's not all, though. No, there's more.

You have elderly family members who you are responsible for getting to doctor appointments, making sure their bills are paid, food is in the refrigerator, medications are taken, and you scream, "STOP!"

Oh no, but there's even more…

You're working on continuing your education, perhaps while dealing with your own health issues. Your husband announces to you at the very last minute that his office is having a dinner TOMORROW and he's responsible for providing a dish, which you know, of course, you will have to prepare.

The kids announce to you that they each have upcoming events over the weekend. Guess what? Not only are you to take them to the events, you're also the chosen driver for some of the other kids.

You scream at the top of your lungs, STOP! I have had enough".

I could go on and on with many different scenarios, but I will stop here. You get it, and you question yourself. You ask yourself, "How in the world am I expected to have some peace while all of this is taking place?"

I'll tell you how. This is something that I will likely repeat throughout this book. Establish some BOUNDARIES. Let your family members know, in no uncertain terms, that you are not a robot, and you cannot drop everything at the spur of the moment to cater to their needs. This should start with your immediate family and then extend it to other family members and friends.

Let people know that because you're not just sitting, twiddling your thumbs, waiting for their next emergency to occur, but you are *actively planning* your time and taking *proactive* approaches to maintain your peace. We tend to have a propensity to allow the situations of others to take precedence over our own peace. That needs to stop now.

Give people a heads-up that from this day forward, you will not rush to their aid as doing so causes disruptions in your peace-filled life. They may not like it initially, but later some will learn to respect you because you have finally begun to respect yourself, your time, your talents, your resources, your peace of mind.

Yes, it can be done. You can live a life of peace regardless of what may be going on around you. We teach people how to treat us. Start teaching them a new way. You'll be glad you did and begin to live a peace-filled and peaceful life.

CHAPTER THREE

GOOD HEALTH-*Regina G. Mixon*

"Beloved, I wish above all things that thou mayest prosper and be in health, even as thy soul prospereth."
(King James Version 3 John 2)

As you can see from the scripture, it is God's will that we are in good health. It is the will of God that we are able to run our race, pursue our purpose, and the only way we can do this is by being healthy.

When I talk about good health, what exactly do I mean? I am talking about spiritually, mentally, emotionally, physically, socially, and financially. I will primarily focus on the spiritual and physical aspects, touching slightly on some of the others. Finances will be dealt with in a subsequent chapter.

Addressing the spiritual aspects first, a person can be as close to God as they CHOOSE to be. Some say that God is not with us, or He doesn't hear and answer their prayers. That is not true.

Some say, God does not even exist. That is false.

Some ask, if God were here, why would He allow so much pain and suffering?

I say that God is very much real, He never leaves nor forsakes us, and He often *allows* things to happen in this world for correction and prayerfully, for repentance to take place.

How can you begin to have good spiritual health? Start by reading your Bible. Next, you should try prayer, and watch God work on your behalf. Now, this doesn't mean that God is a genie, nor does it mean that He will provide instantaneous results. It *does* mean that once you start to actually read and believe the word, God will move on your behalf. Once you begin to pray and do it consistently, EXPECT God to answer your prayers. Don't look at your watch, tapping it saying, "Okay God, it's been a week and you have not shown up." His time is not our time, but He is an on-time God.

Get into a good Bible-based church where the word of God is taught by men and women of God that are called, chosen, anointed, and appointed to preach and teach His word. Ask questions. Participate in Bible studies. God called and chose these people for a reason—to help us. Don't ignore the gifts He has placed inside of them to help you.

Fast. Fasting is an act that is pleasing to God as we seek Him for guidance and direction. Fasting means denying ourselves of something we love, sanctifying ourselves by going before Him in prayer and meditation for a period of time. The most common form of fasting is turning down one's plates or going without foods and liquids, except for water for a designated period of time. During this time, you are connecting with Him through prayer, praise, meditation, and worship.

There are other fasts as well. Some choose to use the Daniel fast, while others fast from social media or television, or telephone calls, or whatever it is that they are led to abstain from by the Holy Spirit.

Listen. Contrary to many beliefs, God does speak to us. Prayer is not a monologue but a dialogue. Get still and listen to hear what the Spirit is saying to you. God is our constant companion; He walks with us, and He talks to us. Sadly, many people often choose to say that "something said" as opposed to "God said" or the "Holy Spirit said or led me to do this, that, or the other."

Now granted, be mindful of the fact that every voice we hear is not God. We speak to ourselves, the enemy speaks to us, and the

Holy Spirit speaks. I often remind myself of the fact that on my right side, whispering in my ear is the voice of the Lord saying, "Do the right thing according to my word." On my left side is my own voice or that of the enemy saying, "Oh no, it's not going down like this. Do the wrong thing. Tell them off. Slap her." We each have those voices. The word of God says that His sheep hear his voice and a stranger they won't follow. Learn to know His voice. He will blow your mind.

Let's now shift and talk about physical health. We often neglect this part. Why? Many reasons, one of which is we just cannot or will not say no to others and yes to ourselves. We have been neglectful in our duties as it relates to taking care of our physical bodies. This has to STOP!

"What? know ye not that your body is the temple of the Holy Ghost which is in you, which ye have of God, and ye are not your own?" (*I Cor. 6:19 King James Version*) We cannot afford to misuse and abuse our physical bodies. We can no longer afford to batter and abuse our own bodies. The price we pay for neglecting our bodies is all kinds of sicknesses and diseases; stress, and feelings of hopelessness. We MUST do better.

We have one body that, like anything else, wears out over time, but we can do some things to preserve these physical bodies we're in. We have the tendency to think that we have plenty of time to get our health together, yet we suffer from high blood pressure, diabetes, heart conditions, and a plethora of other medical issues due to neglect.

Now is a pivotal moment for you who are reading these words. Now is the time for you to decide you are worth it, to stop procrastinating, to stop thinking that one day you will get it together. Later just might be too late.

We must change our modalities and thoughts as it relates to caring for our physical bodies.

Did you know that everyone has 24 hours in a day? I know you did. My point is we have to choose what we do what those 24 hours. We get to choose what we do with them. We decide. Isn't that amazing?

Let's see, we need a minimum of seven to eight hours of rest. That leaves us with 16 hours. If we break that down into keeping first things first by spending the first 30 minutes to an hour a day reading our Bibles, studying, in prayer, and meditating on the word, that leaves us with 15 hours and 30 minutes.

Let's say, for example, we decide we are going to meal prep for the day. If we don't have a designated day each week to do so, and that takes roughly an hour. we still have 14 hours and 30 minutes left.

Break it down further: you must shower, get dressed for work, get the kids off to school, make sure hubby is taken care of, and that takes an hour and a half. We still have 13 hours left. Say we work an eight-hour job, that leaves us with 5 hours. Studying for school, extracurricular activities, homework with the kids, etc.- say that takes roughly two hours. There are still three hours left. You mean to tell me, at some point during this three-hour window, you are unable to carve out some time to exercise? Yes, you can!

Why should you do this? How can you do this? Because you realize that self-care is not a luxury nor is it selfish, it is a priority.

DISCLAIMER: The above schedule I've given you is in by no means a way to live your 24 hours. I used it to illustrate that making yourself a priority and your spiritual and physical health important, a priority, can be done.

A great example of the absolute necessity of self-care that I often refer to is following the instructions we're given before a flight takes off. If you are traveling with a child, before covering the child's nose and mouth with an oxygen mask, place one over your own nose first. In the event the plane starts to descend or even crash, there may not be time for you to put your mask on *after* you've put someone else's on. The same holds true in life. We have tried to be all things to all people, placing ourselves last, and it's time to stop.

I have been so guilty of doing a lot of the things I am sharing with you. I had to learn a lot of the lessons the hard way. We are important. We are worthy. God wants us to live long lives, and (are you ready for this), for many of us who choose to cast dispersions and doubts on God, asking Him, "How can you be so slow?" "Why aren't you helping me to do this?" He is! He is speaking loudly to you, me, and so many others through the penning of this and similar books, through pastors, coaches, mentors, etc.

He is speaking to us saying he wants His best for us. The question is are you listening, or have you closed your hearts and minds to hear what the Spirit is saying to you? Hmmm?

The Bible tells us to be slow to speak and quick to listen. Scripture tells us that today, if you hear His voice, harden not your hearts. Is your heart hardened by past experiences? Have you hardened your heart because of negatives spoken over you? Have you hardened your heart due to lies being told on and about you? Have you hardened your heart because in the past, you screwed up, and you refuse to forgive yourself?

Has your heart been hardened by selfishness? Oh yeah, you were hurt in the past and now you have taken a vow to never, I mean NEVER allow yourself to be hurt again. Guess what? The harsh reality is you are now hurting yourself.

Let me share briefly about the importance of your mental and emotional health. This is all a part of and connected to the scripture mentioned at the beginning of this chapter.

Before I dive into this, please tell me why some tend to think that seeking counseling is a sign of weakness? Why do people think God chose those people? Seeking counseling is a sign of strength, strength enough to say, "I can't do this alone." Strength enough to say, I need to talk with someone that can help walk me through this process, an impartial party that has no objective but to serve and assist me." God chose these people to *help* us.

An awful lot of people that are on the edge, with a little bit of assistance from a mental health specialist, a therapist, a coach, a mentor, a pastor, could likely move from jumping off a cliff or the edge, to breaking through and breaking free.

Many marriages and other relationships would likely be saved had there been proper counseling. Please don't frown on getting help. The life you save may be your own.

I have, for years, believed in seeking outside help. Believe me, it has worked wonders for me, causing me to see some things in a different light. Sometimes we are too wrapped up in the problem to see a clear solution. Get help as often and long as you need to break free. You're worth it!

CHAPTER FOUR

FINANCIAL FREEDOM — Regina G. Mixon

Financial freedom is attainable. As with anything else, it requires a desire to be debt-free, along with discipline, determination, and patience. The Bible tells us that plans fail for lack of counsel, but with many counselors they succeed. It further states that where there is no vision, the people perish, and lastly God's people are destroyed for lack of knowledge.

I can only imagine that you are now saying you have screwed up so bad in the past it would take an act of God to straighten out your finances. No, it takes your faith, your works, your patience, and your determination. Really, how bad do you want it?

Your next question or excuse may concern the unexpected bills that may pop up-- the medical expenses, car repairs, a huge utility bill, or something else that is totally beyond your control. Let's face it, things happen, but that fact should not deter you from becoming debt-free. It can still be done. By the inch, it's a cinch, but by the yard it gets hard.

The very first thing one should do is establish a budget. In addition to your regular monthly bills, include miscellaneous items such as dining out, trips to your barber or beautician, getting manicures and pedicures. Now, we all know that there are some things that will be with us forever. If you own a home or rent, you will always have utility bills.

If you have a car, there will be registration fees, insurance, smog checks or annual inspections, repairs and so forth.

Who here knows what their credit score is? Who regularly check their credit report to find out what's on it? Who knows what their FICO score is and how many different credit reporting agencies there are? Who knows how negatives affect your credit ratings?

Who knows the credit reporting agency most used by many lenders to see if you are credit worthy? Who knows how they rate you? Remember the word says His people are destroyed for lack of knowledge?

Who knows how to get negative items removed from your credit report? Who knows how to get erroneous information removed from your credit report? Who knows why it's so important to become financially literate?

Let me just share here right now, I do not profess to know it all nor to be the expert as it relates to credit repair. Hopefully, many of you have not gotten to the point where you need credit repair but are reading this to take proactive steps to prevent the need for credit repair.

I can honestly say, in my early years, I was clueless about handling credit! I bought whatever I wanted, when I wanted, without even considering a budget. During that time in my life, if I had checks, I would write one to pay for a purchase then try to "catch" it later or place the money in the bank before it would hit the bank. That cost me a lot.

If I had credit cards, I would charge them to the max, not realizing that by doing so was negatively affecting my credit report. The bad part about it was I was not paying the balance in full before the due date nor did I even focus on making payment by the due date as I knew I normally had an additional 10-day grace period. I often missed that date, too.

I bought a new outfit almost every week whether I needed it or not. I bought items of clothing, pieces of jewelry, suits, perfumes, and so much more, then gave them away like it was nothing. Don't judge me — I know there are some of you out there that were either like me or are currently like I was.

I did not shop at just *any* store, either. No, I had to shop at the finer stores for everything. Champagne taste, beer pocketbook. No, scratch that-champagne taste, water pocketbook. I couldn't even afford the beer.

I gave when I shouldn't have. I'm being totally transparent as I said I would. If one person benefits from my mistakes, then it is worth it.

One day I woke up. In reality, I was broke, busted, and disgusted. I looked around and asked myself the question that many of you ask, "How did I get here?"

I decided that I no longer wanted to live that way. Yes, it starts with a decision. I began to make some changes. I began to check on my credit, bit by bit. I saw my credit score go higher and higher, and I was elated.

I began to look at whether things were a want or a need. I began to shop some of the less expensive stores, still looking for quality items. I established a budget, recording my pay dates, amount to be saved, bills, due dates, amounts due, balances, food, household goods and personal items, miscellaneous items such as those I mentioned above, and last, but definitely first — my giving by tithes and offerings.

I began to say "no" and my God, it felt so good.

You might say, "Good for you". Although, I didn't obtain freedom from debt, my credit score was consistently improving. Don't clap just yet. There's more.

My Lord, then I started pursuing my businesses. Guess what? If you guessed that I went right back in debt, you would be right. I saw my credit increase as I used every available resource I had in pursuing my businesses.

I tapped into the money from my savings account. I tapped into the money in my retirement fund. I tapped into my Thrift Savings Plan. I refinanced my home. I tapped into several different lines of credit and believe this or not, for a while it worked. At first, I was able to manage the debt.

The bottom dropped out completely in 2017. At that time, I had no available resources, friends, or so-called friends scattered, and were nowhere to be found. I could not get a dime from anyone. My income dropped. My businesses flopped. We ended up losing it all. Fantasia said it best in her song "Lose to Win" -- "sometimes you gotta to lose to win again".

I became bitter, confused, angry, frustrated, agitated, irritated, depressed, sick, and experienced practically every negative emotion one could possibly go through. I was in denial. This COULD NOT be happening to me!

Thank God there were a handful of people that God placed in my life who helped me and mine during this time. Those people became family.

Thank God that I had a few biological family members who, once they knew the severity of my situation, stepped in and helped love me back to a state where I could sing The Five Heartbeats song, "I Feel Like Going On."

What I don't want is for you to have to go through any of this. What I absolutely don't want is for you to be blind to the facts. I want you to know that if you are currently living in financial chaos, it is not God's best and it is not His will.

The Word states that wisdom is the principal thing, but in all you get, get understanding.

I have given you a few tips and tools on how you can obtain financial freedom. I also shared with you that I am **not** a financial expert, nor am I qualified in any way to give you more than I offer in these writings.

Connections matter. Connect with an expert. Get some sound advice as to how you can become financially free.

Reach out to a reputable financial planner, coach, consultant, whatever. Make sure you properly vet the person. Everyone who posts on social media or advertise financial services is not reputable. Do your homework.

Oh, I forgot. You may be wondering about my current financial status. Am I debt-free with adequate savings, you ask? How's my credit score now, you ask?

To answer the questions, I am still a work in progress. I will say that my credit score was extremely low after the bottom fell out. If they had a category lower than poor, that would have been me. I can proudly say, my credit score is now in the "good" range. I'm working towards "great".

I can and will say that I want it bad enough that I can't stop and won't stop until it gets there. I can and will say that my savings, though not anywhere near I want them to be, *will* be there. How can I say it so assuredly? Because I trust God, I believe as He leads, guides, and directs me, it shall be done. I am willingly and obediently taking corrective steps to improve my credit, He will do the rest.

I believe that God is a restorer and what He gives back is much more than my family and I ever lost. I trust Him to lead me to the right people, at the right time, to make it happen. Why do I believe this? The scripture says if we delight ourselves in the Lord, He will give us the desires of our hearts. If further states, the steps of a good man (woman) are ordered by the Lord. My daily prayer is, order my steps in your word, dear Lord. I want Him to lead me, guide me every day. Make that yours as well.

Congratulations on taking the necessary steps to gain financial freedom. A good man leaves an inheritance for his children's children. Let's change the narrative.

CHAPTER FIVE

BETTER RELATIONSHIPS-Lavina D. Williams

There are many types of relationships, but the four basic types are family relationships, friendships, acquaintanceships, and romantic relationships. Good family relationships are ideal, but we all know that that is not always the case. Good and bad family relationships can influence all other relationships. It is important to have good role models of healthy relationships in our families, however it is not always possible. You must grow and mature to be the good role model that your family needs to see. Do all that you can do to have and maintain healthy relationships with your loved ones. If that proves too difficult or impossible, make sure that you are right and without fault in the situation. **Do not feel obligated to stay in an abusive relationship or to stay connected to an abuser whether it be family, friend or romantic partner!** You cannot control or change others, but you can always work on being a better you. You can encourage others, but it's ultimately up to them to change and want to be better themselves.

Our relationships evolve throughout the seasons of our lives, but the key is to move with the change and not try to fight against it. Seasons change! We have a season as children, teens, young adult. We get married, have children of our own, etc., if we are blessed to live to see all the expected season of life. In every season of our lives, we should honor our fathers and mothers. Ephesians 6:2-3 says that this is the first commandment with a promise attached, that it may be well with you and that you may live long on the earth. So, obeying our parents in our adolescent season and honoring them in every season afterward determines how many seasons we live to see. If you honor your father and your mother, God will keep this promise to you. There is no limit to honor! You should honor them in life and in death. It is a fact that all parents are not good parents. As hard as it is for me to understand that fact, the Bible doesn't say that we are to honor them *if t*hey are good to us. To honor them means to respect them and do right by them even if they did you wrong. God never gives us the OK to render evil for evil in any case. I want to encourage you, if you had parents that may have failed you or did not show you the love that you needed, to forgive them even if you don't have a relationship with them. Forgiveness is your first step to true healing. Honoring your father and mother is not an option and withholding forgiveness is not an option. Jesus said in Matthew 6:15 (*NLT*) "But if you refuse to forgive others, your Father will not forgive your sins." That's also a promise!

Many of us carry so much baggage because of hurts that we have suffered and held on to. We hurt because we refuse to heal, and we refuse to heal because we don't want to fully pardon the person who hurt us. Holding on to offenses does not hurt the offender, it hurts you.

For example, one day my husband said something that ruffled my feathers. What he said would not have bothered me so much if my mind had not traveled back in time and recounted a similar incident from years ago.

It was truly a minor offense, but the memory of the former incident clouded my mind. Immediately the Holy Ghost said, "Forgetting those things which are behind," (Philippians 3:13,14 *KJV*) I said, "Lord, I'll forget it." Then I asked Him, "Lord what if it just happened?" He said, "Put it behind you"! The scripture in its entirety says, Brethren, I count not myself to have apprehended: but this one thing I do, forgetting those things which are behind, and reaching forth unto those things which are before, 14 I press toward the mark for the prize of the high calling of God in Christ Jesus. If you don't put those offenses behind you, they tend to get in the way of your progress. I visualized myself reaching over the things, the things that were in my way when I had the power to move it. Put that stuff behind you! And when you put it behind you, don't look back. Forget it! Out of sight, out of mind. Forgetting is not just failing to remember, it is also putting it out of your mind, ceasing to think about it, or consider it. When your spouse or any of your loved ones hurt you, the devil comes right along and reminds you of every little thing they ever did to you. That's how you know it's the devil—he will always remind you of the bad. The Bible says that love keeps no record of wrongs so file that stuff away in the "Let it go" file! Forgive and heal.

To have better relationships you must be a better person yourself. You may be asking, How can I be a better person? Well, first you have to humble yourself and face the reality that you are not the only one that matters in the relationship. Let go of your pride and love wholeheartedly. Life is so precious and when it's over, there are no do-overs.

As my sons grew in age, I had to learn to let them grow up. When the time came for them to leave the nest, it proved to be more difficult than I had imagined, especially when it was time for my youngest to move out. After realizing that my child-rearing season was over, and the last one of my babies had left, I mourned quietly for about a year. During that time, my oldest son had begun to distance himself from me and I was totally unaware of it. When I realized it, I was very hurt and I really didn't know what to do other than to pray. We were not estranged, but our relationship was strained. I had to let go of any pride that tried to rise in me because my relationship with him was more valuable than self-righteousness. It took some time, but the Lord opened a door for us to reconnect. I decided that I would not allow the devil to keep us at a distance from each other. I reached out and I made myself available to him whenever he needed me. For all mothers and fathers that may be facing this, don't let the devil win. Sometimes we lose focus when they don't do what we want them to do. A mother messaged me on social media upset that her daughter was rebelling against her. She said that she believed that she was looking for a reason to move in with her boyfriend. I told her don't try to fight her and push her into making a bad decision, but instead love her more. If she still leaves, she can't say that it was her mother who pushed her away. Love is patient and kind. Love is not jealous or boastful or proud or rude. It does not demand its own way. It is not irritable, and it keeps no record of being wronged. (1 Cor 13:4-5 *NLT*) Sometimes the right thing to do is the hardest thing to do. One has to wonder; how many relationships could have been saved if we had just showed love instead of rudeness? One has to wonder, if we had just been patient and not flown off the handle? Jeremiah spoke the words of the Lord, "Yea, I have loved thee with an everlasting love: therefore, with loving kindness have I drawn thee." (Jeremiah 31:3 *KJV*) Love draws!

There are times when it seems that our children need us more and then there are times when it seems that they need us less, but if you find yourself too needy for their attention and affections, you will wind up disappointed a lot. So, find something to do, but always make time for family. In my transition from full-time mother of school-aged children to mother of adult children, who live in various parts of the country, the Holy Ghost helped me to see that I had a new season to face and embrace. Embrace it, I have! My relationships with my sons have changed, as they should have. I respect them as men, not just my sons.

Get an understanding!

I had been spending a lot of time with one of my family members, but then her situation changed, and we weren't spending very much time together anymore. I was a little hurt because I felt left out, but the Holy Ghost said, "You don't know what she is going through."

So, I had to get my emotions in check. The lesson I learned from that situation was that we can be too dependent on others to love us "just right" by the way they treat us, or according to how much time they spend with us. The fact is, people can only love us as much as they are capable of, or at least as much as they want to. It was unfair of me to expect that she would always have time for me when she had other things going on. I often ask the Lord for wisdom and revelation, so He is always teaching me something new. The Lord must be the most important person in your life, then you will not have a need to pull on your loved ones so much for love. We all need love, but no earthly person can love you as completely as the Lord can. He began to teach me about love, giving, and receiving it. For instance, I felt like my husband did not love me like he should. I would be so hurt when he got angry with me because there was no consoling when he was angry. So, I would run into the arms of the Lord and cry and just be comforted in His love. He would console me and tell me He loved me. He was teaching me that no one could love me as completely as He does so, I had to cut my husband and my family some slack. Of course, I know my husband and my family love me, but I was counting the way they treated me as love, but the truth is, many times others treat you in accordance with how they're feeling at the time. If you are having a bad day, you know that one harsh word can cut like a knife, so be mindful of how you interact with people.

Above all, have fervent and unfailing love for one another, because love covers a multitude of sins [it overlooks unkindness and unselfishly seeks the best for others] (1 Peter 4:8 *AMP*). Your love for others should be passionate, intense, and hot like lava! It should be so enveloping that even if you are mistreated by others, they should still feel love from *you*. To show love when you don't receive love take the supernatural power of God. If you don't have that kind of love, then you need go into the presence of God and get it. Your love should cover their shortcomings even if it is not reciprocated. I know that can be hard to do, but that is how we should love one another. That's how Jesus loves. Even as he was being beaten and ridiculed, He gave His life for his attackers and for us. He said, "No man taketh it from me, but I lay it down of myself." (John 10:18 *KJV*) He didn't get so fed up that He called those 12 leagues of angels to deliver Him, He went all the way for love. He overlooked their unkindness and unselfishly sought the best for them and us. He died for love, and He rose in love for you, so everything you do should be in love. Your love should cover others even when theirs doesn't cover you. Jesus said, "By this shall all men know that ye are my disciples, if ye have love one to another." (John 13:35 *KJV*) Love is the sign. People should know you by your unfailing love.

How bad do you want better relationships? If you truly desire better relationships in your life, you must humble yourself and love like Jesus commanded you to do." The depth of your desire for better relationships determines how and how *deeply* you love others.

CHAPTER SIX

YOUR MINISTRY — Lavina D. Williams

When I started the Facebook live broadcast called "A Study in the Word" it was a step of faith and obedience. It may seem like a light thing to some but, I felt like a little girl wearing adult shoes. It seemed that I had taken on an enormous responsibility that was for someone more qualified. I had not shared these feelings with anyone but the Lord. One day, at a prayer meeting the Lord spoke these words through a Prophet, "You didn't choose ministry, I chose *you* for ministry." Those words gave me the confirmation and push that I needed. The Lord always sends encouragement when you need it. No matter how you view yourself, God sees you in a different way. Gideon viewed himself as poor and little, but God said that he was a mighty man of valour. **You are who God says you are.** Just because you don't see it doesn't mean that it's not truth and just because others don't see it doesn't make it a fantasy. Some people will not acknowledge the greatness in you even if they see it. David was in the field with the sheep while the others were sanctifying themselves at Samuel's request. When the ceremony began, no one bothered to call David into the house. That says to me that he was the least expected of his father's sons to be anointed king. God often chooses those who others would never choose. It is better to be chosen by God than elected by men. David was out of sight when Samuel came to anoint a king in Jesse's house, but he did not miss his appointment with destiny, and neither will you. **In your time of waiting, you may be overlooked and discounted by others, but don't be discouraged.** When I confessed my call to preach, I knew the main area of my ministry would be evangelism. I was so excited that God had given me a name for my ministry, and that He had given me the words to put on the gospel tracts to pass out, but before I could even get it off the ground, I was discouraged by an elder who was very influential in my life.

Evangelism was my purpose, and the word of God was my passion, but there were no preaching assignments coming my way. My phone was not ringing! I knew that it was a time of waiting, but it was somewhat disheartening to see that the other ministers were being used and I was just sitting. Like David, I would encourage myself in the Lord. I felt like I was ready to blaze the trail, but looking back, I realize that I was not ready. Had I been in high demand then, I would have messed up a lot of people, including myself. I was not mature enough to handle all that ministry would call for or for the demons that I had seen come into the services when my pastor and first lady ministered. You must be anointed for that type of warfare. God knew that I wasn't ready, so He had to hide me to prepare me for the next level of anointing. He will hide you during a season so that He may process you and prepare you for what He has already ordained for your life. Gideon had no idea what the Lord was about to do through him when he was out there threshing wheat by the winepress to hide it from the Midianites. David was hidden out in the field shepherding his father's sheep until his promotion came to him. You may not be popular or talented, and you may not be a Gideon or a David, but you are *somebody,* and you have the potential to do great things for the Lord. If you surrender to the will of God, He will use you.

A Word of Prophecy

God is making somebodies out of nobodies! He is calling people from the back to the front and transforming those who are sanctified into people of importance in the marketplace, in government, and in regions, both nationally and internationally! He is calling the obedient to do what others who have held positions will not do! He is preparing some of you for elevation from the valley, to take your position on the mountain! God is raising up voices to be heard in these last days. He said that He has gifted you for purpose and you have been entrusted with a special assignment. Don't get comfortable because you must be ready when it is time to move. Prepare for elevation, prepare to be used by God, and don't limit your faith. Just as God was preparing David to be king when he was keeping his father's sheep, He has been preparing you for your next season. Therefore, *Enlarge the place of your tent and let them stretch forth the curtains of your habitation, spare not, lengthen thy cords, and strengthen thy stakes, for you shall break forth on the right and on the left and fear not, for you shall not be ashamed. (Isaiah 54:2 NKJV)*

Get ready for your next! In your season of hiding, you should be preparing for what God said. You don't have to run after the promise, run after Jesus. Whatever God has ordained for your life, will come to pass. All you have to do is be obedient and He will lead you right to it. *Run after Jesus!* No one will encourage you to step into the call and assignment like the Lord.

Genuine men and women of God will inevitably experience rejection. Rejection is a part of the process. It can really feel like isolation, but it is working for your good. Being rejected helps you to realize that the love of Jesus and the sweet communion of the Holy Spirit is more important than anything else in this world. People can be fickle, but God is always faithful. I was rejected so much, I almost got used to it. I began to expect rejection. When the Lord transitions you to a new level, everyone will not be happy for you. Some people won't accept you on any level other than where you used to be. God has a way of weeding out people in your life. There were some people that I wanted to connect with, but God wouldn't allow them to connect with me. There were other people that I tried to connect to, but the Lord said, "No!" If people reject you, just remember that Jesus was rejected, too! Some rejection is God's protection. So, don't let it discourage you or stop you from soaring. God will send the right people to help you to push and birth the greatness in you. He will also separate you from people you may have grown used to in your former season, but may have become adversaries in your new season! Everyone is not destined to go with you but, go anyway!

Everyone wants to move to a new level, but do you really want to go through the preparation it takes to reach that new level? The preparation process for your elevation is tailored just for you. I can't tell you what your process will be since there is no standard pattern for everyone. However, I can say that whatever it is, it will press the oil out of you. Preparation is part of the crushing process that accompanies the move to greater heights. Crushing does not feel good, but it works for your good. Olives have to be crushed to get the oil; grapes have to be crushed to make wine. Olives and grapes are edible and good as food, but the process of crushing increases their values. You must suffer the crushing. It maximizes the anointing on your life. The anointing comes at a price, but the rewards far outweigh the cost. David went up to sacrifice to the Lord on the threshing floor that belonged to Araunah. Araunah offered David the threshing floor for free, but he said to Araunah, "No, but I will surely buy it from you for a price; nor will I offer burnt offerings to the Lord my God with that which costs me nothing." So, David bought the threshing floor and the oxen for fifty shekels of silver (*2 Samuel 24:24 KJV*). Anything that you offer the Lord has to cost you something or it means nothing. Dr. J.H. Jowett said, "Ministry that costs nothing accomplishes nothing." The anointing costs. Revelation costs. You must go through some changes to change lives, atmospheres, and regions. The oil is valuable, and it costs. Jesus had to experience Calvary and go through agony to be glorified forever. He had to suffer to save you.

Transition is also a part of the process of preparation, and it can be rough. It can even make you want to turn around and go back, but the door of the old season shuts as soon as you take the step toward the new season. During this time, it can seem like everything around you is changing! As a very young girl, I noticed that some of the girls I knew, who were not much older than I was, had started to change. They started to act more mature, and I didn't understand it. They had begun to change in preparation of their new season. They could not go into middle school with an elementary mindset. Their next level required a change. Each level prepares you for the next level, so don't get comfortable where you are. The seasons will change, and you have to adjust to the season.

I believe the transformation from "nobody" to "somebody" is likened to the changing of the guard. God is moving some up and He is moving some people out. We saw this transformation start in 2020 with the onset of the pandemic, but it is not completely fulfilled yet. A "somebody" is a person of importance, a person of authority and influence. Some of those who are in positions of influence will retire, be rewarded for their service, then be replaced. Jeremiah 1:10 says those the Lord are raising up will have authority to root out, and to pull down, and to destroy and to throw down, to build and to plant. He is making you a "somebody" to give you influence so that you can sow His precious seed in the hearts of men and people will hear you when you tell them about Jesus. He is developing the gift in you and that gift will make room for you and bring you in the presence of great men. You must know how to act when you get there, so remember these four things highlighted from 2 Corinthians 4:

> **Remember your assignment.** 2 Corinthians 4:1 *KJV* Therefore seeing we have this ministry, as we have received mercy, we faint not. Dismiss all distractions that come to get you off track. You must stay focused on your assignment. When you preach, say what God tells you to say whether it is a word of encouragement, correction or judgment and keep it moving! Don't bring the line to the people, but bring the people to the line. Your obedience and allegiance are to God not people! Don't allow anyone or any situation to pull you from your assignment. Some people are your

assignment, but not all, so rely on the Holy Ghost to sharpen your gift of discernment so that you don't waste precious time and oil. Get your emotions in check and remember what God said, not how people made you feel! Study to shew thyself approved unto God, a workman that needeth not to be ashamed, rightly dividing the word of truth. (2 Timothy 2:15 *KJV*) When you fall in love with Jesus, you should also fall in love with the Word of God. You have to study in order to preach and teach. Jesus is revealed in the Word of God. You must learn of Him in order to tell others about Him. He said in Matthew 11:29, "Take my yoke upon you and learn of me;" There is no way that you can know everything about Him, but as you study, He will reveal Himself more and more. Jesus is the living Word and studying and meditating on scripture will draw you closer to Him. Every Christian should be a Bible reader and certainly, every preacher should read and study the Bible. By far, the most important thing you must do to enjoy a successful ministry is to spend quality time with the Master. Jesus always slipped off into the wilderness to pray to the Father. You must have a prayer life.

Let your character back up your ministry. 2 Corinthians 4:2 *KJV* But have renounced the hidden things of dishonesty, not walking in craftiness, nor handling the word of God deceitfully; but by manifestation of the truth commending ourselves to every man's conscience in the sight of God. Work always to be a person of integrity and do not use the gospel to benefit your own interests. You represent the one who called you, so make Him look good! You must understand that you have to answer to God, and that your ministry is nothing if Christ is not the center and pinnacle of your life. God will expose the hidden heart of man, whether good or bad. God loves His people and those who are real will also love His people!

Remain humble. 2 Corinthians 4:5-6 (*KJV*) For we preach not ourselves, but Christ Jesus the Lord; and ourselves your servants for Jesus' sake. 6 For God, who commanded the light to shine out of darkness, hath shined in our hearts, to give the light of the knowledge of the glory of God in the face of Jesus Christ. It is not about you! There are so many people who are caught up in the fame of their own person. Jesus is the star, no one else! Paul says we are servants for Jesus' sake. Jesus himself did not come to be served but to serve. Are we greater than Jesus? Greater is He that is in us than he that is in the world. The light is in us to reveal and glorify Jesus to others, not to glorify self. 2 Corinthians 4:7 (*KJV*) *But we have this treasure in earthen vessels, that the excellency of the power may be of God, and not of us.* You have the God-given power to pick up the Bible, but you will only receive His power when you receive the Word, believe the Word, and do what the Word says to do. In the Word, we have power and authority. We are nothing without Him. When you humble yourself before God, He will exalt you.

Your destiny is tied to God. 2 Corinthians 4:14-16 (*KJV*) *Knowing that he which raised up the Lord Jesus shall raise up us also by Jesus and shall present us with you. For all things are for your sakes, that the abundant grace might through the thanksgiving of many redound to the glory of God. For which cause we faint not; but though our outward man perish, yet the inward man is renewed day by day.* God called you for His people. He predestinated you to do what you do for His glory. Don't let go of Him. *Whatever God has ordained for you is not to bring you glory but to bring Him glory.* Never forget your assignment and to whom you must give account. King Saul was king of Israel, but he started to do things his own way and disobeyed God, so the kingdom was stripped from him. Don't get stripped! God loves His people, and He loves obedience. When

God calls you to serve His people, He gives you a heart and love for His people. Just as the people that come to Christ will be presented to Him, so too, will you.

Anyone can serve in a ministry, but there are certain roles in ministry that God has to specifically call and anoint you for. Whatever the responsibility, if everyone does their part, the ministry is sure to be successful.

CHAPTER SEVEN

YOUR MARRIAGE-Lavina D. Williams

Marriage is a beautiful thing, and it is to be treasured and respected by both parties. Understand that marriage is a sacred, honorable covenant that was created by God for a man to join in with a woman. Any marriage that is not between a male and a female is not a blessed covenant.

You can really learn a lot in marriage if you are *willing* to learn. Not only should you be willing to learn, you should be willing to work at maintaining a good, strong relationship with your spouse. My husband and I were both previously married. When we got married, I thought things would be easy because we met in church, and he was really nice; so was I. But he and I had different ideas about our roles in the relationship. His ideas were more traditional and mine were more modern, to say the least. He was expecting me to do things in certain ways, and I was doing those things in ways I thought would work better for us. Needless to say, we ran into more than a few problems. We *didn't,* however, run into any problems that prayer could not and did not fix. I prayed about every little thing that was lacking in our relationship, because little problems can turn into big problems. I believe in the power of prayer. The bible says the effectual, fervent prayer of the righteous avails much. I know my prayers were availing because every time I went to the Father about any issue and-there were-many, I saw a change. Although I felt like he was the one that was wrong most of the time, the moment I began to pray, I was convicted to also pray for myself. My prayers would go something like this, "Lord, I'm mad right now! He was wrong, but Lord, I may have been wrong, too! Help him to treat me right and help me to treat him right. Even though I felt he was wrong, I acknowledged my shortcomings also, and I always saw a difference after I prayed.

The Holy Spirit began to teach me how to humble myself and let me just point out that I was disobedient once or twice. My husband would make me so upset, and I would inform God that I was going to tell him off, but the Holy Spirit would tell me to hush so I just had to eat those words and be quiet. For me, obeying the Spirit of God was more important than getting the last word in an argument. I want to keep the fellowship of the Spirit in the bond of peace.

As I humbled myself, my attitude and how I responded to my husband improved. I began to learn more about my husband and our marriage. The Lord helped me to understand we grew up in different families, with different parents. We had different experiences, so he was bringing what he had learned to the marriage, and so was I. No matter what we already knew, we had to be willing to learn how *God* wanted us to be if we wanted to make our marriage work. There must be a willingness by both parties to make a marriage work. I'm not talking about just staying together and despising one another, I'm talking about having a good relationship.

With humility comes wisdom. I submit to the Lord, and He helps me to submit to my husband. I know that the modern woman may have a problem with submitting to her husband, and believe me I understand, but when I changed the way I approached and responded to my husband, he changed the way he approached and responded to me. Sometimes you have to quietly take the lead in order to effect change. If you lead with kindness and gentleness, it will most often be reciprocated. That is the kind of leading that no husband will refuse. You can teach people how to treat you by treating them the way you want to be treated. Yes, we're talking about applying the Golden Rule. To be honest, I had to get over myself. Acting like a spoiled child, throwing fits didn't really work well, and it is not the behavior of a wise woman. I began to apologize quickly for things said and done, intentionally and unintentionally. An apology is sometimes all that a person needs to hear in order to heal. Just taking ownership of something that you did or said, that hurts your spouse or anyone else, can make a great difference in the health of the relationship. Remember, the word "but" is not included in a sincere apology. When you add that word, "but" you are basically taking the apology right back. "I'm sorry but…" is not the proper way to start an apology.

In marriage you must become vulnerable. Oh my, I never would have been able to do that. without the Lord's help! When my husband and I joined together, we brought our fortified walls with us! Anytime friction arose between us, the walls would go up. I couldn't get behind his walls and he certainly wasn't going to get behind mine! I never liked it when he would shut me out, or shut down altogether. It never felt good being closed out, but it always felt safe when I ran behind my own walls. Realizing and accepting my own insecurities helped me to identify more with my husband. I realized that he was doing what he knew to do because he didn't want to be hurt again. So, what did I do? I had to tear my own walls down first. Those walls are places to hide behind. When my husband would retreat behind that wall, I wanted him to stand with me and fight against the devil who was trying to bring division into our marriage. I needed him to stand with me. The thief does not come except to steal, and to kill and to destroy. (John 10:10 *NKJV*)

He will destroy your marriage and your family if you don't fight. The devil will try to tear down or pervert anything that God joins together. You must make up your mind not to give place to the devil and be willing to fight for what is rightfully yours. I decided that if I couldn't live a life with the person that I love outside of those fortified walls, then what was the point of us being together? So yes, again, I had to tear my walls down first. I was finally able to fully open my heart. I decided that if I sustained any hurt, I just sustained it, but I wasn't going to live a life behind "protective" walls. It felt like a form of bondage, and I was ready to be free and open with my husband. In order to have a healthy relationship with your spouse, you have to remove all barriers to communication and communion.

If a husband loves his wife like Christ loved the church, then submission will never be an issue. Jesus gave His life for the church. He was fully committed and He proved it. To love like Christ means to love with your life. His love was not conditional, or He would not have given His life for us. The bible tells the wife to submit to her own husband. Marriage is a lifetime commitment and should not be entered into lightly. I believe that if you get married, you have a responsibility to do all you can to make it work. When you put Christ first and your spouse second, you have a winning hand. There is no room for pride and selfishness in marriage. Pride cannot love like Christ and pride will not submit. Submission does not include ownership. Submitting to your spouse doesn't make you a slave. You don't relinquish your rights to any person, and/or give anyone complete and total control of you. Living life under those conditions constitute living a life in bondage. Do not submit to abuse or complete control. If you are a victim of domestic violence or are being held captive by someone, please pray and seek help so that you can get out safely. If you are in need of help, contact the National Domestic Abuse Hotline at 1.800.779.7233 or text the word START to 88788 from your mobile phone.

A Wise Woman Builds Her House

I remember as a very young adult hearing an elder encourage other wives not to talk about their husbands in the street. That was a simple teaching that I have never forgotten. There are things about your husband/wife that no one should know except you. Sharing private information sometimes sparks another person's curiosity and gives the devil ammunition to blow up in your face. Don't help the enemy destroy the gift that God has given you. You should respect your marriage enough to keep private things private. Every wise woman builds her house: but a foolish one tears it down with her hands. (Prov 14:1 *BSB*) A wise woman is not out there all by herself holding up beams and nailing them together. She is building on the inside with her husband. To build means to form by ordering and uniting materials by gradual means into a composite whole. A wise woman is taking care of her house — her husband and children. She is an example of a good wife to her children, she is encouraging her husband, and she fosters a place of peace for her family. Jesus Christ is the foundation that a wise woman builds upon. A house built on a bad foundation will eventually start to crack, both inside and outside. If the necessary repairs are not taken care of, in time, the environment becomes a danger to its inhabitants. A wise woman builds a safe house because she seeks the Lord's direction about every detail, and she builds according to the plan of God. Jesus Christ is the only foundation strong enough to build a marriage and a family on.

You know a wise woman when you see her because she is busy building her house, but a foolish woman is busy pulling her house down. If you tear down your husband and family, you are also tearing down yourself, which is self-destructive behavior. It takes skill to build with intricate detail! It's better to be a builder than a demolitionist! People give credit to builders, but no one inquires about the person who tears a building down. The people in your household see you more than anyone else does, so you shouldn't live to impress only the people on the outside, but you should live in order to make a difference in the lives of the people in your home. The things your children *see* you do act as greater teachers than the things you say.

While I didn't start this chapter with love, it is certainly the most important component in a marriage! People are drawn together most commonly by physical attraction, but if true love never forms in the relationship, there is nothing to work with when trouble comes. Recently, I watched an episode of *Little House on the Prairie* where storekeepers, Mr. and Mrs. Oleson, had a fight that was so bad, they separated (within their home), and everyone in town came to witness the "separation". Mrs. Oleson was set on taking her children and moving back to her hometown, and Mr. Oleson has no intention of stopping her. The Ingalls, though, put together a plan to help them remember the love they had for one another. When all was said and done, love prevailed. When everything else was falling apart, their love was still standing strong. Bears all things, believes all things, hopes all things, endures all things. Love never fails. (1 Cor 13:7-8a *NKJV*) And now abide faith, hope, love, these three; but the greatest of these is love. (1 Cor 13:13 *NKJV*)

CHAPTER EIGHT

YOUR BUSINESS-Regina G. Mixon

Starting a business or a ministry is not for the faint-hearted. If you believe starting a business or ministry is something you are *purposed* to do, let me be the first to tell you that you will have to have PATIENCE, and most of the time, you will need a lot of it.

How Bad Do You Really Want It?

At the onset of a business and/or ministry, there is this huge excitement. You've taken the proper steps to get your business going, done your research and development, and you're good to go…or so you think.

You have taken the proper classes, established what you believe to be a great network, and you're good to go…or so you think.

You've gone to the crème de la crème, the experts in various fields to help you to make it happen, and you're good to go…or so you think.

Papers are all in order, and you have your core group, your team players, and you're off…or so you think.

My point is that every step along the way in this journey comes with some good and some bad. One cannot be weary in well-doing or just stop in the middle when things are not going so well. One cannot become discouraged when the plan doesn't work or when the team members you thought you could totally rely on start to drop off, one-by-one.

Starting a business can and should be very exciting! Starting that business or following His direction to start that ministry is something that should make you proud. That is why you started the business or ministry, right?

Look, if you start a business solely for the sake of making money, I encourage you to rethink the whole thing. Our businesses should be ones we are deeply passionate about and something that will help change the lives of others. Money is a byproduct of starting, operating, and maintaining a successful business.

If God granted you the vision to start a business, let Him lead, guide, and direct you. Don't be so focused on money that you fail to see the lessons along the way. Get a full, clear understanding of why God gave you the vision and what you are to do with it.

Of course, there will be highs and there will be lows. There will be seasons of plenty and seasons of lack.

There is a scripture in the Bible that says, except the Lord builds the house, they labor in vain that builds it. Going a bit further into the Word, it tells us that for everything there is a season, a time to build, and a time to tear down. Know which season you are in. Pray and trust God to build your business, your ministry. Don't allow your building to be in vain.

Starting and operating a successful business or ministry can and should be very rewarding. Just think of the opportunities that will follow your starting and operating a successful business or ministry. One of the most satisfying will be your chance to provide stable employment for others. Another, and of the most gratifying will be the opportunity to leave a successful business to your family. You will have the opportunity to train many – those who will accept the assignment of your delegation – to be your successors. That is priceless!

The opportunity to have a family-owned and operated business that serves the needs of others, provides a source of livelihood for others still, and will be part of your legacy is again, priceless.

Building businesses takes time, sometimes, numerous sacrifices, and you may hear the word "no" a lot. You may knock on 25 doors or 200 doors before you finally get that one "yes" that will catapult you to the next level.

I've read and heard it said that most overnight successes take about 20 years. Imagine that! This is not to discourage you in any way, but rather to encourage you. You will move from glory to glory, from one level to the next, to the next and so on. A quitter never wins, and a winner never quits. You are in it to win it, right? It's in your DNA, right? So, once you've put your hand to the plow, how can you ever look back?

How bad do you really want it? It's time to P. U. S. H. - Prepare Until Something Happens and by all means, have Patience Until Something Happens.

Patience is a virtue. If we focus on practicing it daily, and are fed on the word of God, you will find that patience is a great asset to you on the journey to not only becoming an entrepreneur, but becoming a successful one whose efforts will be passed from generation to generation. It takes time.

I have likely made every mistake there is as it relates to business. I went to some who gave me good, sound advice, and then went to others who had never started a business asking their *opinions*. The people who offered good sound advice were the ones who were already doing the things I wanted to do, and most were experts in their fields. Was I insane because I still wanted to pursue entrepreneurship? Yes!

I would always say, don't go to someone who's never owned a home and ask what steps to take to purchase one. They don't know! Don't go to someone who's never in their life owned a vehicle or never worked at a car dealership and ask the proper steps to purchase a vehicle. Ludicrous!

To do either of those things would be ludicrous, yet sadly, I am guilty of having done that sort of thing before. And I paid a price that was very costly which could have been avoided had I only listened to those wiser than I based on their prior experiences and taken the proper steps. Blessed is the man that walketh not in the counsel of the foolish or those that don't know.

CHAPTER NINE

TO BREAK AN ADDICTION-Regina G. Mixon

Then he answered and spake unto me, saying, This is the word of the Lord unto Zerubbabel, saying Not by might, nor by power, but by my spirit, saith the Lord of hosts. Zechariah 4:6 KJV

For the sake of clarity, in this this chapter, references to addictions will not be limited to those relating to substance abuse. An addiction can take many forms. Substance abuse, people-pleasing, self-doubt, low self-esteem, bowing to the opinion of others, and many other debilitating, self-destructive habits and conditions are unhealthy addictions that must be broken in order to live freely. Addictions and conditions that need to be overcome and bound range from overeating – eating ten honey buns a day – to drug addiction, alcohol abuse, nicotine addiction, snuff-dipping, tobacco chewing and so many others. Habits such as procrastination or constantly entering toxic relationships must be dealt with and overcome.

What causes addictions? There are many different reasons people become addicted to destructive behaviors and habits. One of them is learned behavior. We say things like, "My mother did it. Her mother did it before her, and her grandmother, and so on did it. So, it has to be right." Wrong!

Other reasons addictions occur is due largely to ignorance as it relates to starting destructive patterns or behaviors in the first place. Many don't like to use the word "ignorance", but ignorance in any matter is due to a lack of knowledge about the consequences of one's actions. It may be years later, but those initial and subsequent actions will eventually develop into an addiction, and the question becomes, "How do I break free from this?" At some point, the addicted person may find him or herself thinking, I've done it so long, there is no way I can break free, but that's not true.

I honestly don't believe that anyone raises their hands on career day in school, and when asked the question, "What do you want to be when you grow up?", will respond, "I want to be an addict. I want to be obese. I want to be incarcerated for most of my life. I want to be unhealthy. I want to choose the wrong relationships repeatedly. I want to be lazy and do absolutely nothing. I want to be a prostitute." No, I don't believe any make conscious decisions to CHOOSE to be addicted to any of those things as a child.

So, what happened? Maybe someone lured us into thinking that the lives we currently live is as good as it gets.

Maybe someone entices us to take that first toke or drag on the drug or cigarette without telling us we could later die from a heart attack or stroke or any number of things due to that one bad decision. TV commercials have always made things appear to be glamorous, but they don't tell us the bad consequences that we could experience later.

It could have been something as simple as wanting to appear "grown" at an early age to impress our so-called friends. Your first bout in jail got you street creds, but little did you know it was the beginning of a vicious cycle and recidivism would become your lifestyle.

That fast dollar you made using your body as a sex object later brings you pain and pure hell. In and out of jail, HIV, AIDS, and other sexually transmitted diseases were not even thought about, and God forbid the fact that you could have been maimed or murdered. Those things never even crossed your mind. Sheer ignorance.

I've said it before, and it bears repeating: God's people are destroyed for lack of knowledge. Ignorance equals a lack of knowledge, so you see why some addictions or habits develop.

After so much hurt and pain, sometimes it is our normal proclivity to start to think that there is no hope for the situation to ever turn things around. The lie detector determines that is definitely a lie. Now, I know you may be saying by now, "This is my story, so how do I break this vicious cycle and break free?" That's what I am here to address.

Let this book be the catalyst to help you jump start your life and finish strong. Let this be the refresher or reminder you need that you **can** break those destructive habits. Let it be the beginning of an amazing ending.

Okay, so how do you do this? I often refer to the Bible as I am a believer. "For as he thinketh in his heart, so is he: Eat and drink, saith he to thee; but his heart is not with thee." Proverbs 23:7 (*KJV*) Replace any negative thoughts you have about who you are with positive affirmations like, Yes, I can do better! Yes, I can break this addiction, whatever it may be. Yes, I can change my circle, if necessary, in order to live a better life.

CHANGE YOUR THOUGHTS AND CHANGE YOUR LIFE

Begin to say, "Yes!", to God first, then to yourself. Make a commitment, a vow, to God and yourself that you will not be defeated, you will turn your life around with His help, and that you will be an overcomer.

Know that this is something you cannot do alone. As the scripture at the head of this chapter states, it is not by might, nor is it by our own power, but by His spirit. Invite him into your situation. Ask God for His help. Ask God to give you the strength that you need to endure as He is delivering you from the destructive patterns. Wait patiently on him. Sometimes, things don't happen in the timeframe we think they should, but they that wait upon the Lord shall renew their strength. Wait on Him.

In the spirit of transparency: I have dealt with breaking so many addictions in my life and I am so grateful that God did not remove everything at one time, even though I prayed for that to happen. I likely would have gone into a state of shock. I say that God, however in his infinite wisdom, started pruning away things bit by bit.

I've shared with you my destructive financial habits. Now, allow me to share that there was a time when I absolutely hated water and rarely drank it. It's a wonder my kidneys did not fail me. To God be all glory. For the biggest part of my life, I drank maybe, *maybe*, a bottle of water a day. It was only a year or so ago that I began to really understand the importance of drinking more water. Initially, I increased my intake of water when I learned of the overall health benefits it provides, including improved kidney functioning, healthier skin, and many other things. Later, I did drink more for weight loss purposes.

Let me clarify something. I had read and heard the many benefits over the years, but I just didn't like water. It was tasteless, and I thought "yuck!"

Guess what? Now I drink approximately one gallon of water each day and love it. What happened? I changed my mindset about drinking the water, and as a result my habits changed. Now, don't get me wrong, I still drink Diet Coke sometimes, but my main beverage each day is water.

I still attribute the desire to begin drinking the water to God's leading and guidance. Because of this, I give Him all the praise and know that He is working out absolutely everything as it relates to my well-being, in His own time and His own way.

Do you realize that being a workaholic is a destructive habit? Yes, I was guilty of that as well. I felt enormous pressure to get things done now, not realizing the to-do list was perpetual and never-ending. I had that "get it done now" mentality.

I learned that all work and no play make Jack or Jill bitter and unfulfilled and that is totally out of God's will. So, to my fellow workaholics, God wants us to have balanced lives. Lighten up! Now, this does not by any means that we should procrastinate on doing things. This *does* mean we must plan for rest and relaxation, family, and fun activities. We must develop a plan of action that takes into consideration all of these things. *That* is having a balanced life.

Hopefully, by now, you know that it is not impossible to break destructive habits and begin the process of building better ones. By now, you should know that with God, nothing is impossible. You first have to have the desire to change, be willing to change, and always be obedient to the promptings and leadings of the Holy Spirit. Just because it hasn't happened yet does not mean it won't happen. The Bible tells us if we delight ourselves in the Lord, He will give us the desires of our heart. Patience is an absolute must.

Many of these habits did not begin overnight and likely won't end overnight, but I assure you if you stay the course, they will be broken. That's not my promise to you, it's God's.

Do I still have some self-defeating habits that need to be broken? Yes, I do. I say to you as I say to myself, it's all in God's timing. I have prayed and prayed and done some of everything in my power to break some of my bad habits. I remind myself that it's not by my own might nor by my own power nor is it in my timing. I remind myself that it is all in His hands and I trust Him to do what only He can do. You can as well.

CHAPTER TEN

TO LOOK GOOD FROM THE INSIDE OUT-Lavina D. Williams

Women and beauty go hand in hand! Women are naturally beautiful, but we like to enhance what the Lord has given us. Cosmetic surgery used to be for the rich and famous, but now, any of us can name several people that we know who are not rich, who have been under the knife. I don't knock it because I could stand to have some nips and tucks myself, but there are so many risks involved. I often wonder, *Is it really worth it?* There is so much pressure to look a certain way. I promise this is not a bash on anyone, but are we too focused on the outside? Some people are working on looking like Barbie and they are messed up on the inside. I know that people have different reasons for enhancing themselves, but I believe that first we should enhance the inside. Improving the inner woman (or inner man) should be more desirable than working on our outward body. No matter what some people do to themselves, they will still not be satisfied.

Jesus told the scribes and Pharisees in Matthew 23:27 (KJV) *Woe unto you hypocrites! For ye which indeed appear beautiful outward but are within full of dead men's bones and all uncleanness.* The Scribes and Pharisees thought they were better than everyone else, they were self-righteous. They worried more about the appearance of uprightness than actually being righteous. Jesus called them out. In my experience with the Spirit of Christ, He calls those things to your attention so that you can get them right. The Bible says that open rebuke is better than secret love. Jesus was not just talking to one person, but to all of them.

Investing in yourself is not just spending money, but spending time in the Word. The Word of God is the only thing that will transform your mind. It will teach you who you are in Christ. You are a son/daughter of the King.

Peter says to adorn the hidden man of the heart, in the incorruptible [ornament] of a meek and quiet spirit, which in the sight of God is of great price. An ornament is a thing used to make something look more attractive. God is attracted to inner beauty. You should desire to be more attractive to Him than to anyone else. I have seen some really beautiful women with really ugly attitudes. Their character was not hidden behind their pretty face. Whatever is in you will come out at some point. The real beauty should be on the inside. Your heart will expose your true character.

Inner beauty is developed as you grow in the grace and wisdom of God! Meek and quiet women are not on display, but they are certainly noticed. They are beautiful in God's sight, and they are pleasant to be around. We try to impress people, but God is the one to impress. He is not impressed by what impresses us. God doesn't see like man sees; He looks at the heart. So, the makeup, expensive clothes, the body enhancements, only make the outside look good, but the ornaments of a meek and quiet spirit increase your value. The hidden man of the heart is what we need to invest in and beautify. Hidden means to be kept out of sight; concealed. The hidden man of the heart is hidden from human eyes but is revealed through conversation and actions. The heart is very important — we hide the word in our hearts and the Bible says from the abundance of the heart the mouth speaks. You can't hide your heart behind outside adornments, everything is naked before God! He sees everything. God is looking at your heart, He sees the hidden man of the heart. No man can see your heart, but your actions display the purity of it! Sin is conceived in the heart and birthed through your actions. That is why you must meditate on the word of God, day and night!

Proverbs 31:30 (KJV) says that favor is deceitful and beaty is vain: but a woman that feareth the Lord, she shall be praised. Outer beauty fades, but inner beauty is imperishable. It is not diminished by time, but it is recognized, and sets you apart from others. You should want to look better on the inside bad enough to allow the word to transform your life!

CHAPTER ELEVEN

A CLEAN HOUSE-Regina G. Mixon

Now you may be wondering what in the world does having a clean house have to do with anything. Allow me to explain.

I know you all have heard the phrase "cleanliness is next to godliness." At least, I believe that to be true. What does it truly mean? How can I have a clean house? Why is this even important? I have kids, so how can I do this? They are so unruly and get into everything. I work a full-time job, am a student, have a business, lead praise and worship on Sundays and now you're saying in addition to all of this, I have to clean?

Why am I really addressing this in this writing? It is biblically sound. Titus 2:4-5 says the older women are to teach the younger women. Verse 5 talks about being keepers at home. Being keepers at home includes keeping a clean house.

I know you might be saying, "Wait a minute Regina, I'm not through just yet!" I have a HUSBAND too! You know all that goes along with taking care of him? Cooking, making sure he and the kids are fed, homework is done, participating in not only my husband's activities, but the kids' activities. They're in EVERYTHING! Help me, because I truly don't know WHAT to do." Lord, I get it, believe me I do.

Now, why is it important to have a clean house? Does it really have to be squeaky clean at all times, or can we have that "lived in" look?

Let's look at your priorities as well as where you are in life. If you're a single woman with no kids and have tons of things taking place at the same time, it may be totally different than that of a single mother or a married woman, or a married woman with kids. This is not a one-size-fits-all message as there are many different scenarios.

If you are a seasoned woman, perhaps you are divorced or widowed. Maybe you live alone or have been tasked with raising young grandchildren. You might find that your adult children have returned to the nest for a season. Whatever the case may be, you may be asking, "Is having a clean house really at the top of my list of priorities?

It should always be. Clean does not necessarily mean spotless at all times. Let's face it, no one is looking to live in a house that is more like a museum. Most of us want the house to be full of love, joy, laughter, and sometimes a little messiness. We want it to be enjoyed.

In the case of adult children returning home, there should be some house rules as far as the cleaning schedule. It should be clearly laid out who does what and when. You should **not** be solely responsible for the cleaning of the house. Every adult in the household has a role to play. Get united. A house divided shall not stand, and if necessary, get it in writing so there is no confusion as to who does what and when they should do it.

If your adult child(ren) returns to live with you along with their child(ren), or if you have the responsibility of raising your grandchild(ren), their roles in keeping a clean house should be dependent on their age(s). If they are infants up to age three, then of course establishing rules might be a bit ridiculous. By the age of four, they should start to have some responsibilities such as picking up their toys. Make it a game. Say something like, "Let's clean the toys up and put them away and see who gets it done faster."

As they continue to age and figure out it's not a game and no longer fun—shift to more responsibilities, such as taking out the garbage or making their beds, and continue the process. We are responsible for training our children/grandchildren and it is best to start them early in life.

Side note: Just because our adult children may move back in with us does not mean they should not share in other responsibilities, including assistance with the payment of the bills or an agreed upon amount for rent and utilities, food purchases, cleaning products, etc. Know that it is not your responsibility to do their laundry and cook and prepare their meals unless you want to. You are also not the built-in babysitter. Make it clear at the onset.

Now, to address those of you who are single with no children and live alone or are at home with parents. I say to you, there is absolutely no excuse. Does this mean that your house must be always immaculate? No, it does not, and I only have four words for you, you can do it!

Now, let's help those who are newlyweds and are faced with continuing education, no children, and a mountain of other tasks to do. I have the same four words for you, you can do it!

I have three additional words for you, yes you can!

Finally, here are two words for you: No excuses!

To those that who are single with children, I have four words for you – you can do it!

Follow the same steps outlined above if you are a grandparent having to raise your grands. It can be done.

For those of you who are divorced or widowed, and living alone, your ability or capacity to do the work to maintain a clean house will be largely determined by your age and/or medical condition. Nonetheless, my four words for you are the same as they are for others: you can do it!

Now, your "how" might be a bit different, as you may have to hire someone to come in once a week should a medical condition prevent you from being able to clean your home. Otherwise, if you are in a great position to do it yourself. My six words to you are, how bad do you want it?

To the married women who are faced with wearing many, many hats—wife, mother, doctor, lawyer, PTA President at not one, but two schools, soccer mom, Sunday School Teacher, a career professional, chef, driver, cook, choir director, aspiring entrepreneur, you name it: we have run out of excuses.

A final thought to be reminded of is that a cluttered house, like a cluttered mind, leads to serious depression. Did you know that? If you have ever watched the show *Hoarders*, many experienced severe depression and began the process of hoarding due to some traumatic experience. Of course, initially they refused any offer of help and were in deep denial of their hoarding. They considered themselves collectors.

Many, after receiving some professional counseling, went on to come to accept the fact the reason the hoarding began, the fact that it was a problem, and began the "separation of items" process. Some appeared to be elated after having cleared their house for the first time in many years, and sometimes even decades. Although the show doesn't present it, I can only imagine the sigh of relief the participants release as they are finally able to let go of some of the weight in their lives and make a fresh start.

I am not saying you are a hoarder. I only use this as an illustration. When you think you cannot do something, think again. Look for ways that work for you and know that **you can do it**!

With any change, we go through various stages of death or dying to self. We go from denial, thinking the situation is not that bad, to ultimately accepting the situation, which should lead to taking corrective action. You CAN do it!

CHAPTER TWELVE

YOUR JOB-Lavina D. Williams

I have worked several low-income jobs throughout my life because I had only a GED. I have had some factory jobs that paid better, but for some reason or another I didn't stay. This is more a message to you on faith than a how-to-snag-the-right-job. Earlier, I told you in chapter about my act of obedience and getting the job at the church nursery. When I worked at that church nursery, I felt the power of prayer working in my life. Not just my prayers, but I felt the prayers of that church for me. I had entered a place of greater faith, and it was really a time where I felt a change in the atmosphere around me. It was like an aligning was taking place in my life. I was at the place that God ordained for me to be. He reserved that job for me so that I would be aligned with His will and purpose for my life. The job you have or the field that you desire to work in should not just be about the income. You should go where God tells you to go. If it doesn't pay what you think you deserve, I promise you that God will make it enough. He will give you favor with men and favor is more valuable than money.

I had never wanted to work in an office because it seemed so boring. But I had gotten to a point in my life where I was ready for a change, so I began to profess that I was going to get an office job. I went shopping to buy myself some clothes for my office job and I later enrolled in business college. Because of financial aid issues, I had to either amend my federal income tax, or I could not finish, so I did not finish. Not long after that I had my office job, but it was only a temporary job until the young lady on leave came back. There was another young lady that was recently hired who was not doing so well in the position, and another lady who just didn't care. I remained humble and I was careful what I said about them and their work because only God knew how it would work out. When you try to lift yourself up and show up others, they may end up getting what you thought you deserved, and you get your walking papers. I ended up keeping the job and both the ladies were relieved of their duties. I knew God had placed me on that job. Jesus promised me that if I asked anything in His Name, He would give it me. I prayed and I believed God for that job! I had no idea how He was going to do, but I trusted Him. I know now that He put the desire in me to work in an office. He knows the thoughts that He thinks towards you and me thoughts of peace, not of evil to give you or me an expected end. The business that I work for was taken over by another business and everyone had to reapply for their jobs and interview all over again. When I went for the interview, all of the unit leaders were there, choosing who they wanted on their teams. I felt like I would be hired, but I wasn't really worried about it because God had told me that I wouldn't have to work much longer, so I was excited at the thought of it coming to pass. I did get rehired, received an increase in pay, and after a year I got a promotion. As these promises began to manifest in my life, I went to my vision board as I often do, and read the prophecies spoken over my life! Hebrews 10:23 *(KJV)* Let us hold fast to the profession of our faith without wavering (for He is faithful who promised). Whatever God promised you, hold on to your faith until you see it come to pass. God has proven Himself to be faithful. It pleases Him when we trust Him. Even when we don't see it, He's working, as the song says. He never stops working! I went from a cubical to a private office.

There are some other promises in my prophecy that have not fully manifested yet, but they are coming as well. The businesses are coming, the money is coming, the new house is coming, the latter rain is coming. I'm expecting! When I was pregnant with my children, I didn't wait until they were born to prepare for them. I started to prepare for them when I found out I was going to have a baby. I made room for them, I prepared names for them, I had their clothes, diapers, and bottles in expectation of them coming into my life. You have to make room for the promises that God has made you. Until they get here, they should be fresh on your mind. You have to let God know that you are looking for it and you are ready for it. Now faith is the substance of things hoped for, the evidence of things not seen. Hold on to your faith until it manifests in your hands. Even when it looks like it is taking a long time to come, don't change your words. Keep speaking positive and keep speaking faith. Without faith it is impossible to please God.

A job is not your source, God is your source. I have seen people working at McDonald's doing better than people working at General Motors. If God is with you, you will prosper wherever you are because your provision comes from Him. If you want greater in your life, start confessing it and believing God for it to come to pass. There are no limits in God. He is unlimited. The limits were broken when He gave his only begotten son. He that spared not His own Son, but delivered Him up for us all, how shall He not with Him also freely give us all things? (Romans 8:32 *KJV*) If He gave His only begotten Son for you, what will He *not* give you? What will He withhold from you? God can do anything!

My sons have a lot of faith. One of my sons really has high expectations when it comes to getting jobs. Wherever he applies, he applies for the highest position. I used to try to tell him to just get in the door and work a while and they will promote you. Well, that did not discourage his faith. He still believed for supervisor jobs, management jobs and because of his faith he started walking into those jobs. He has confidence that what he sets out to do, he will do.

Begin to document your prophecies and start a vision board if you have not already so that you can go back and read it, and be encouraged by what the Lord has done and will do in your lives.

Father I pray for each reader's faith to increase and that they will see the impossible made possible, In Jesus's mighty name, Amen.

CHAPTER THIRTEEN

AN ABUNDANT LIFE-Regina G. Mixon

*"The key to abundance is meeting limited circumstances
with unlimited thoughts."*
Marianne Williamson

Abundance or an abundant life is our birthright. Some don't seem to realize that. In John 10:10 (*King James Version*) Jesus says, The thief cometh not, but for to steal, and to kill, and to destroy: I am come that they might have life, and that they might have it more abundantly. It is the Lord's desire that we live an abundant life.

What exactly is abundance? One dictionary defines it as:

- A very large quantity of something

- The state or condition of having a copious quantity of something; plentifulness

- Plentifulness of the good things in life; prosperity

If we connect the Bible with the dictionary's definition, we will find that God wants us to have more than enough of every good and perfect thing; not just live on "Barely Get Along Street" or just to survive, but to thrive.

His desire is that we are blessed beyond measure so that we, in turn, can be a blessing to others. Are you living the abundant life? Do you believe that you can? I am here to let you know if you are not, you most assuredly *can* live an abundant life.

As I talk about abundance, am I strictly talking about living a prosperous life as it relates to material things? Not at all, but material abundance is also a promise of God. In this writing, I talk about total life abundance which consists of spiritual, physical, and material abundance.

Spiritual abundance is when one appreciates and values the gift of life, health, mind, body, and soul. It is not focused on material blessings or abundance as it gages its focus more on the spiritual aspects of life: love, joy, peace.

The dearly departed Wayne Dyer wrote, "Abundance is not something we acquire. It is something we tune into." I couldn't agree more. Spiritual abundance is not about acquisition of material things, but rather a deeper appreciation of that we have, a desire to serve others utilizing the knowledge, skills, gifts, and talents that we are blessed to have, and the freedom to gift to those who God leads, guides, and directs us to.

Author Laura Emily (The Happiness Coach) writes that "Abundance is already within you. Let it out."

It can be so easy to let abundance overflow from your life to the life of another. The question then becomes, are you willing to do it? If not, what's holding you back?

Staying connected to God through the daily reading of His word, prayer, meditation, attending church services from His anointed and appointed leaders, and/or watching inspirational messages helps one to stay spiritually connected which yields huge rewards as it relates to spiritual abundance.

Yes, you can have it. It is yours when and if you reach out and grab it.

GOD WANTS US BLESSED SPIRITUALLY!

Physical abundance. What does it mean to have physical abundance? This subject has already been covered in-depth in a previous chapter. However, know that having physical abundance deals with having our physical bodies, our temples, in the best possible shape as it can be. There are many preventative or proactive steps we can take to do this.

To repeat, exercise, proper rest, healthy eating, ridding ourselves of toxicity - toxic relationships and habits, drinking plenty of water are all apart of having physical abundance.

If we find ourselves in a state of reacting due to negligence on our part, we still can get on track by following prescribed medications and treatments by our physicians, seeking guidance and counseling from reputable and respectful sources, and starting to develop better habits as laid out above. It is **not** too late to turn it around. God wants us blessed physically.

Material abundance. The Bible has much to say about material abundance. All throughout it lets us know that God not only wants us to be blessed spiritually, nor does he want us only to be blessed physically, but he wants us blessed in every area and all aspects of our lives.

Read John 10:10 again.

God wants us blessed materially. Yes, the Bible does state that the poor will be with us always, but if you know that you know that you know that you are one called and chosen to be blessed to be a blessing, then this does not refer to you.

If you know that you know that you know that God has given you visions and dreams for not only you and yours, but resulting in your impacting the multitudes, then this scripture does not refer to you.

Now we should not have possessions or any abundance merely for the sake of being greedy or hoarding these things. Luke 12:15 KJV "And He said unto them, Take heed, and beware of covetousness: for a man's life consisteth not in the abundance of the things which he possesseth." The Bible also asks, what does it profit a man to gain the whole world yet lose his own soul?

We must be careful how we allow abundance to affect us. Always keep in the forefront of your minds that God blesses us to be a blessing. Know that this does not mean that we are to give hand-outs to people, but rather hand-ups as we are led by the Holy Spirit to do.

Whatever you do, do not apologize for living an abundant life and do not allow anyone to put you on a guilt trip for doing so.

Many will have opinions as to what you should do with the resources God has given you. Many will have opinions as to the lifestyle you choose to live as a result of the blessings God showers like a continual stream of rain. Many will do whatever they can to get you sidetracked, to cause you to lose your focus on how God leads you and have tons of opinions.

Many will think you're not doing enough for the people, for the community, for the family, for your friends (or so-called friends). I am saying this loud and clear: DROWN OUT THE NOISE AND HIT IGNORE, IGNORE, IGNORE, DELETE, DELETE, DELETE!

Many don't realize that with each of these — spiritually, physically, and financially you have paid a hefty price to get where you are. The same ones who so readily voice their opinions when and as God elevates you are most likely the same ones that dropped you as you were going through.

This is not about holding grudges, or any unforgiveness issues at all. It is about knowing that the first part of John 10:10 states that the thief comes not but to steal, kill, and destroy. Recognize the enemy and shut him down.

HOW DO I GET THE ABUNDANT LIFE GOD HAS PROMISED ME?

There is a scripture found in Isaiah 1:19-20 *(King James Version)* that states, If ye be willing and obedient, ye shall eat the good of the land. But if ye refuse and rebel, ye shall be devoured with the sword: for the mouth of the Lord hath spoken it.

So, one part of getting and living the abundant life is being willing and obedient.

Another scripture which readily comes to mind is found in John 15:7-14 (*King James Version*). 7 If ye abide in me, and my words abide in you, ye shall ask what ye will, and it shall be done unto you. 8 Herein is my Father glorified, that ye bear MUCH fruit, so shall ye be my disciples. Read for yourself in your leisure the remaining verses. The bottom line is, God wants us blessed!

CONCLUSION

As you read this book, it is our prayer that you read it with an open mind and a receptive heart. Not only does God want to you be saved, healed, delivered, and set free from any bondages or chains that are holding you back, but so do we.

Pray the Prayer for Breakthrough at the end of the book. Ask God to awaken the king or queen in you, and help you to be the person He created you to be. Quit sitting, settling for the crumbs from the table when God has called you for greater. Quit sitting on the sidelines when God has chosen you to be the head and not the tail, above and not beneath, the lender and not the borrower.

Get your house in order: your spiritual, physical, financial, emotional, mental, social. Do it today.

Get your house in order as you are destined to win! You are destined for greatness! Your destiny awaits you! Greater is calling you. You are a generational curse breaker! You are anointed and appointed for such a time as this!

Will it require work? Yes, it will!

Will it require faith? Yes indeed!

Will it require patience? Absolutely!

Will you be misunderstood? Definitely!

Will you sometimes have to walk alone? Indeed!

Will you have to step outside your comfort zone and connect with new people while leaving some of the old ones behind? Most assuredly!

Will you have to take a proactive stance as opposed to constantly reacting? Yes sir, yes ma'am.

Will it be worth it in the end? YES!

God is a Way Maker, Miracle Worker, Promise Keeper, Light in the Darkness! God wants HIS BEST for YOU!

The question is: "How Bad Do You Want It?" We mean, REALLY want it. If you're like us and you are willing to go the distance and be obedient as He leads, then…IT'S TIME TO P.U.S.H. and give birth to those babies inside of you. It's not about us, but all about Him. It's not about us, but changing generations, breaking generational curses and beginning generational blessings. It's not about us, but rather God and His glory.

So, tell us, how bad do you want it? Better yet, allow your actions to speak; don't tell us, show us.

Blessings,

Regina G. Mixon & Evangelist Lavina Williams

ABOUT THE AUTHORS

Regina G. Mixon

Regina G. Mixon is a 9-time author hailing from Minden, Louisiana. Regina is a Professional Certified Life and Purpose Coach. Regina helps women aged 18 and over who have been battered, abused, and broken, break through barriers that have kept them stuck, break free, identify their purpose, and begin the process of pursuing their purpose by taking manageable steps. Working with Regina assures one of purpose, passion, and positivity!

Regina is a mother, grandmother, and great-grandmother.

Regina is a faithful member of the King Solomon Baptist Church in Sibley, Louisiana, where her Pastor is Dr. Rodney E. Williams. Under his leadership she has grown by leaps and bounds.

Using her God-given gifts, extensive knowledge of what it takes to grow, and a genuine desire to see others flourish, Regina Mixon is here to serve those who are ready to elevate their lives to a new, exciting level. Regina is a Purpose Coach, Start-up Business Consultant, Author, Speaker, and Minister that uses her own life experiences to help enrich the life experiences of those willing to learn. She is highly passionate about helping women to awaken the passionate, fervent woman inside herself - the woman that God created her to be. "First and foremost, I want these women to understand that God loves them so much. My goal is to help them learn to love themselves and to realize their worth. I teach them to understand that even their biggest dreams are not out of reach and that their pasts do not determine their futures. "My passion is to help women C. L. I. M. B.—Create Lives/ Leaders Implementing Manageable Balances" she says.

As a woman who has endured many hardships in life and has spoken with countless others who have or are currently suffering in silence, Regina decided to form Women Destined to Win International, one of her businesses under God's Storehouse Ministries' umbrella, a 501©(3) organization. Her overall goal is to help women, aged 18 – 64, understand that they are here for a purpose. "I want women to understand that God loves them, and for them to identify themselves in Him, and to begin the process of pursuing their purpose with passion and intent. Once they realize how valuable they are to God, they will come to realize a new, strengthened sense of self-worth."

God has taken Regina on what she calls an extremely long journey, which has allowed her to unlearn many things she was taught or "learned" behavior she adopted along the way. Breaking habits, people-pleasing, injurious financial habits, health, relationships, and so much more. "Those unhealthy, disastrous habits lasted more than 20 years," she says.

Realizing that what she went through was not just for her but also for her to help others as well. She understands that just like her, many women were not properly taught, and because of this, have made numerous mistakes. Many have had unhealthy childhoods or were victims of molestation, rape, physical abuse, verbal abuse, teen pregnancies, divorces, poor financial planning, etc., wore masks, and many other hardships in life. "God wants us to live an abundant life! He wants us whole!"

Follow her on Facebook @ Regina Mixon and Women Destined to Win International

Website: https://womendestinedtowininternational.com
godsstorehouseministries.org

Evangelist Lavina D. Williams

Lavina D. Williams is a wife, mother, grandmother, evangelist, teacher, preacher, paralegal, and a conference and crusade host. She grew up in a small southern town, Minden Louisiana and now resides in Heflin Louisiana with her husband, Deacon Tommy Williams.

Evangelist Lavina, under the leadership of Dr. Rodney E. Williams, of Sibley, Louisiana, preached her first sermon on September 11, 2011. She has since graduated from Caddo Theological Seminary in Shreveport, LA. Her ministry has been blazing a path for men, women, boys, and girls to come to Christ and accept Jesus as their Savior. She has a passion for God's people and for leading them to Christ. Her passion and commune with Christ led to the founding of So Loved Movement. This movement had its beginnings as a tent crusade whose mission is soul winning and equipping God's people for the journey of life in Christ. Its purpose is to minister to the lost in communities and empower the people of God. Her passion for Christ has also led to her hosting the Fire Conference, Pulse & Purpose broadcast on Facebook, and A Study in the Word bible study hosted on Facebook. She is an intercessor and a great supporter of Prison ministry. She is involved in Bible distribution to prisoners and all who desire the Word of God.

You can reach her website @: lavinawilliams.com

Follow her on Facebook: So Loved Movement & Lavina Williams

Subscribe to her YouTube channel: Evangelist Lavina Williams

Prayer for Breakthrough

Father, I acknowledge you and I thank you for who you are, and I acknowledge that you can do anything. Lord, I believe that you are God and besides you there is no other. Father, I acknowledge that I need you and without you I can do nothing. By the authority vested in me by Jesus Christ, I bind up every generational curse, every unnatural soul tie. I bind up every evil scheme and assignment of the enemy against my life. I declare that no weapon that is formed against me shall prosper, and every tongue that rises against me is condemned. I cancel every negative word that I may have spoken against myself or my family, and I declare and take ownership of the blessings that you have declared over me in Your word. Poverty and lack must go, in Jesus's name! I shall prosper in every good thing! I am blessed, my children are blessed, my children's children are/shall be blessed in every generation, my ministry is blessed, my relationships are blessed, my businesses are blessed, and I decree and declare that everyone that I know will come to Christ and receive salvation. Father I thank you for breakthrough in all areas of my life and for peace of mind. Now, Lord, stir up in me the tenacity to PUSH into the new!

Father, I thank you for hearing and answering this prayer, in Jesus Christ's Name, Amen.

Evangelist Lavina D. Williams

www.ingramcontent.com/pod-product-compliance
Lightning Source LLC
Chambersburg PA
CBHW051654060726
47593CB00021B/1091